INTERACTIONS I
A Reading Skills Book

SECOND EDITION

INTERACTIONS I
A Reading Skills Book

Elaine Kirn
West Los Angeles College

Pamela Hartmann
Los Angeles Unified School District

McGraw-Hill, Inc.
New York St. Louis San Francisco Auckland Bogotá
Caracas Lisbon London Madrid Mexico Milan
Montreal New Delhi Paris San Juan Singapore
Sydney Tokyo Toronto

This is an  book

Interactions I: A Reading Skills Book
Second Edition

3 4 5 6 7 8 9 0   DOH DOH   9 5 4 3 2

ISBN 0-07-557524-8

Manufactured in the United States of America

Sponsoring editor: Eirik Børve
Developmental editor: Mary McVey Gill
Project editor: Marie Deer
Copyeditor: Stacey Sawyer
Art director: Jamie Sue Brooks
Text and cover designer: Cheryl Carrington
Cover illustration: Rufino Tamayo: *Wedding Portrait (Retrato matrimonial),* 1967. Oil on canvas, 136 × 195 cm. B. Lewin Galleries/Palm Springs, California.
Illustrators: Axelle Fortier and Sally Richardson
Typesetting: Graphic Typesetting Service
R. R. Donnelley & Sons Company was printer and binder.

CONTENTS

PREFACE
To the Second Edition

INTERACTIONS: THE PROGRAM

INTERACTIONS consists of ten texts plus two instructor's manuals for in-college or college-bound nonnative English students. INTERACTIONS I is for high-beginning or low-intermediate students, while INTERACTIONS II is for low-intermediate to intermediate students. Within each level, I and II, the books are carefully coordinated by theme, vocabulary, grammar structure, and, where possible, language functions. A chapter in one book corresponds to and reinforces material taught in the same chapter of the other three books at that level for a truly integrated, four-skills approach.

Each level, I and II, consists of five books plus an instructor's manual. In addition to the readers, they include:

A Communicative Grammar I, II: Organized around grammatical topics, these books include notional/functional material where appropriate. They present all grammar in context and contain a wide variety of communicative activities.

A Writing Process Book I, II: These books use a process approach to writing, including many exercises on pre-writing and revision. Exercises build skills in exploring and organizing ideas, developing vocabulary, using correct form and mechanics, using coherent structure, editing, revising, and using feedback to create a final draft.

A Listening/Speaking Skills Book, I, II: These books use lively, natural language from a variety of contexts—dialogues, interviews, lectures, and announcements. Listening strategies emphasized include summarizing main ideas, making inferences, and listening for stressed words, reductions, and intonation. A cassette tape program with instructor's key accompanies each text.

A Speaking Activities Book I, II: These books are designed to give students the opportunity to practice their speaking and listening skills in English by promoting realistic use of the language through individual, pair, and small-group work. Task-oriented and problem-solving activities simulate real-life situations and help develop fluency.

Instructor's Manual I, II: These manuals provide instructions and guidelines for use of the books separately or in any combination to form a program. For each of the core books except *Speaking Activities,* there is a separate section with teaching tips, additional activities, and other suggestions. The instructor's manual also includes sample tests for the grammars and readers.

The grammatical focus for the twelve chapters of *Interactions I* is as follows:

1. the simple present tense; pronouns
2. the present continuous tense versus the simple present; *there* versus *it;* the modals *can, may, might, will*
3. nouns; comparison of adjectives and adverbs; the modals *can, could, will, would, may;* the future with *be going to*
4. review; phrasal verbs
5. the simple past tense; *used to*
6. the past continuous tense; infinitives
7. more on infinitives; *should, had better,* and *must;* the reflexive; adjective clauses with *who* and *that*
8. review
9. the present perfect with *since, for;* the present perfect continuous
10. gerunds
11. the present perfect tense with *just, already, yet, still,* and so forth; the superlative
12. review

INTERACTIONS I: A READING SKILLS BOOK

Rationale

Interactions: A Reading Skills Book is based on the idea that people learn to read by *reading.* If the material is interesting and not too difficult, students will enjoy reading and will be encouraged to read more; the more they read, the better they will be at it. The problem for academic ESL students is that they want to read sophisticated material but lack the skills with which to do so.

The solution is twofold: (1) to give students readings that are intellectually stimulating but not beyond their lexical, grammatical, or syntactic understanding; and (2) to teach strategies that make reading easier. The reading selections in INTERACTIONS contain sophisticated material; however, vocabulary and grammar have been very carefully controlled to be at the students' level of comprehension. In addition, the exercises guide students toward acquiring the skills of good readers, skills that make reading both easy and fun.

Vocabulary items presented in one chapter of INTERACTIONS are recycled in subsequent chapters to prevent students from forgetting them. This constant recycling enables students to make rapid progress; their vocabulary will increase dramatically as they use the book, and yet this process won't be perceived as difficult.

One of the biggest obstacles to comprehension in many academic ESL readers is that the grammar is too difficult for low-level intermediate students. They simply haven't learned it yet. In the reading selections of INTERACTIONS, however, the grammar points have been carefully sequenced and appear only as students are likely to learn them. This text is not only coordinated with the grammar text in the INTERACTIONS series but is also compatible with the sequencing in most ESL grammar syllabi.

It should be noted that since this is a *reading* book, grammar is not taught for the sake of grammar. Instead, it is seen as an aid—one of many—to comprehension. Other such aids, or strategies, taught in this text include: guessing meaning from context, increasing reading speed, understanding stems and affixes, making predictions before actually reading, learning to accept some amount of uncertainty, and making inferences.

The fact that the material in INTERACTIONS *looks* difficult but *isn't* allows students to read easily and with a growing sense of confidence and accomplishment. Academic students won't feel that their intelligence is being demeaned by puerile material.

Chapter Organization

Because its primary purpose is to provide instruction in the reading process, INTERACTIONS offers a large variety of exercises and activities directed toward that end. It is left to the individual teachers to choose those sections suited to the specific needs of their students. The following outline lists the different kinds of activities in the four parts of each chapter:

Part One

Getting Started: a prereading exercise consisting of a picture and questions about it; sets the tone for the chapter

Preparing to Read: prereading questions for the students to keep in mind as they read the selection

Glancing at Vocabulary: A list of potentially new vocabulary items from the reading selection that follows, broken into groups according to parts of speech (words later included in the *Guessing Meaning from Context* section are not included here)

Reading Selection: a controlled reading on the theme of the chapter, usually nonfiction, giving practical information

Getting the Main Ideas: a post-reading exercise to help students check their general understanding of the reading selection

Guessing Meaning from Context: specific suggestions followed by exercises on words from the reading selection

Recognizing Reading Structure: exercises focusing on organization of ideas or relationships between ideas

Understanding Details: exercises focusing on specific details of the reading selection

Discussing the Reading: questions that relate the reading selection to the students' lives and allow for conversation

Part Two

Glancing at Vocabulary: vocabulary items that may be new from the second reading selection

Skimming for Main Ideas: an activity that guides students in recognizing the main idea of a paragraph

Reading Selection: the second controlled reading of the chapter, similar in theme to the first but usually somewhat lighter, divided into lettered paragraphs

Inferring: Figuring Out the Meaning (Chapters 10, 11, 12): helps students recognize implication

Viewpoint (Chapters 5, 7, 12): questions that guide students in separating fact from opinion

Discussing the Reading: as in Part One, questions that relate the reading to students' lives through in-class conversation

Part Three

Building Vocabulary: a variety of exercises to help students expand their passive and active knowledge of vocabulary

Study Skills: activities to aid students in acquiring essential skills for academic reading, such as dictionary usage and increasing reading speed. Additional exercises for some chapters appear in the instructor's manual.

Part Four

A section of "realia" (a page from a college catalog, food labels, street signs, advertisements, etc.) accompanied by a short glossary and questions for scanning.

Part Five

Personal Stories: one or two brief fiction accounts based on the chapter theme. Always in first-person narrative form, these stories contain practical information about life and culture in North America for foreign students and immigrants.

Teaching Hints

The following suggestions are designed to help teach the reading strategies used by good readers, skills essential to students' academic success

Part One

Prereading: The skill of anticipation—forming predictions about what is to be read—is an important part of active reading. This skill may be encouraged through the *Getting Started, Preparing to Read,* and *Glancing at Vocabulary* sections. First, have students discuss the picture, answering the questions in the *Getting Started* section. Then read through the *Preparing to Read* questions. Tell students that they aren't expected to be able to answer these questions before reading. Instead, they should keep them in mind as they read. Since teachers disagree on the value of vocabulary preparation before reading, the *Glancing at Vocabulary* section is optional. Students can repeat each item after the teacher, for pronunciation practice, and learn the meaning later, or the teacher might introduce the meaning at this point, before the reading selection.

Initial Reading: Each student should read the selection silently, as this is the most common form of academic reading. The selection should be read quickly, without a dictionary. Encourage students to guess the meanings of new words. Emphasize the importance of simply getting *the main idea*—the most basic of reading skills.

Have students complete the *Getting the Main Ideas* section, which checks comprehension of general themes and important ideas in the reading. Students should complete these exercises quickly, without looking back at the reading selection. The answers can be checked later, after students reread the selection.

The *Guessing Meaning from Context* section is self-explanatory. It contains specific hints and step-by-step exercises on *how* to guess meanings of new words, thereby avoiding tedious and time-consuming trips to the dictionary.

Rereading: Students reread the selection, this time more carefully, focusing on details. Although they might occasionally use a dictionary this time, they should still be encouraged to apply the skills they have learned in the *Guessing Meaning from Context* section.

When they finish the selection, students should check their answers in the *Getting the Main Ideas* section before completing the exercises that follow.

Postreading Exercises: Students will need to look back at the reading selection to better understand its organization as they do the exercises in the *Recognizing Reading Structure* section.

They may also refer back to the selection as they answer questions in the *Understanding Details* section.

Students can actively practice their newly learned vocabulary words as they express their opinions and share ideas in the *Discussing the Reading* section. There are a number of ways in which the questions in this section may be answered. Among them:

1. Ask the questions of the entire class. The advantage to this technique is that the teacher can control the discussion and encourage students to expand on their ideas. The disadvantage, though, is that few students may volunteer to speak.
2. Have students discuss the answers in small groups (three to four people). A representative from each group can then report that group's ideas to the whole class.
3. Have students discuss the answers with just one partner. This technique is conducive to the participation of students who are usually too shy to speak in a larger group.
4. Choose one of the questions and organize a debate on it. Divide the class into two sections, each of which will prepare arguments for its team.

Part Two

The suggestions from the *Glancing at Vocabulary* section in Part One also apply here. Next, have students skim (read quickly) the paragraphs in the reading selection and find the main ideas. They shouldn't use a dictionary but, instead, should try to guess meaning from context. Also, they shouldn't worry about details at this point.

After students reread the selection (Chapters 1–5, 11, and 12), this time using a dictionary where absolutely necessary, they work through the *Inferring: Figuring Out the Meaning* section (Chapters 8–12); completing these exercises necessitates referring to the reading selection to separate ideas *stated* in the reading or *implicit* in it from those not in it at all.

Use the *Interpreting Sentence Structure and Meaning* section that appears in the instructor's manual as needed. The exercises are particularly useful for those classes that still require or want reading instruction on the sentence level. They may be duplicated, distributed, and completed in class or assigned as homework.

The techniques suggested for the *Discussing the Reading* section in Part One may also be used for *Viewpoint* (Chapters 5, 7, and 12). In addition, you might try a role-play activity where appropriate; students will play the parts of different characters from the reading selection.

Any of the suggestions for the *Discussing the Reading* section in Part One may also be applied to the same section in Part Two.

Part Three

Although the *Building Vocabulary* exercises can be assigned as homework, the *Study Skills* section should be completed in class, particularly those exercises dealing with increasing reading speed. To streamline the progression of activities, those sections directed at lower-level students have been moved to the instructor's manual in the second edition. Duplicate and distribute these as needed.

Part Four

The ability to find specific information quickly is an important skill for academic students and is the focus of Part Four, *Scanning for Information.* Briefly go over the short glossary with the students. Then have them answer the questions, individually or in groups, from the information found in the realia. Discourage them from reading every word as they hunt for the answers. Instead, they should run a finger over the page (either down or across, depending on the type of realia) until the answer "pops out" at them.

For the *Going Beyond the Text* section, students, for homework, find a map, brochure, etc. on the theme of the chapter. They bring it to class and share it with the other students, in small groups or with the entire class. It is meant as a brief summary of the ideas and vocabulary from the chapter.

Part Five

The purpose of the selection or selections added to each chapter in the second edition is to provide supplementary reading practice in which students combine and practice the skills learned earlier. Unlike other readings, these may contain a few words and structures not previously introduced; encourage students to figure out this vocabulary and these forms from context and—if they are not essential to the point—to tolerate ambiguity, being content to grasp the general idea. You may also want to use these sections to help students increase their reading speed, using any techniques that prove effective.

Have students read the paragraphs quickly, guessing meaning from context and making use of the specific clues to meaning presented in previous chapters. Giving clues if necessary, help them to express the main ideas in one or two sentences. At first, ask comprehension questions and have the class answer; as students gain proficiency and fluency in reading, encourage them to make up their own questions about the main ideas and important details of the selections. Point out that if they ask the right questions, their answers will result in a kind of summary of the information.

You may want to allow or require students to tell and/or write their own personal stories on the chapter theme and to listen to or read one another's writing.

Changes to the Second Edition

1. A new section, *Part Five: Personal Stories,* has been added to each chapter; these short narratives give extra reading practice and provide practical information about North American culture.
2. Readings and exercises have been updated and revised as necessary.
3. The instructor's manual contains new quizzes for each chapter that can be duplicated and distributed to the students. Also, exercises on "Understanding Details" and "Interpreting Sentence Structure and Meaning" are included in the instructor's manual for selected chapters.
4. The book has been changed visually, with a clearer design and layout. New photos and artwork were included as needed.

ACKNOWLEDGMENTS

The authors wish to express their appreciation to the creative founder and staff of EBI—Eirik Børve, Mary McVey Gill, and Lesley Walsh—the artists Sally Richardson and Axelle Fortier, the production staff led by Marie Deer, the copyeditor Stacey Sawyer, and each other, for a smoothly symbiotic working relationship. Thanks also to Donn Robb, Marlene Sinderman, Ann Snow, and Hamid and Roya Fahmian for valuable suggestions and to Patrick Haverty for a number of brainstorming sessions.

Thanks also to the following reviewers of the first edition for their help on the second edition: Anne Bonemery, James Burke, John Kopec, Linda Levine, Laurie Roberts, and Christine Salica.

E. K.
P. H.

SUMMARY OF READING SKILLS
(Blank boxes indicate recycling and review of previous skills)

CHAPTER	PART ONE			PART TWO
	Guessing Meaning from Context	Recognizing Reading Structure	Understanding Details	Skimming for Main Ideas
1 School Life	definitions after *be*	paragraphing (topics)		recognizing topic sentences
2 Nature	definitions and explanations in parentheses	recognizing the main idea		
3 Living to Eat or Eating to Live?	definitions or explanations in parentheses or after a dash or comma		connecting words: *and, but, or, because*	
4 Getting Around the Community	examples and details		colons (:) and semicolons (;) between related ideas commas after items of a series quotation marks around direct speech	choosing the main ideas (restatement)
5 Housing and the Family	opposites explanations and equivalents		transition words: *in other words, that is, also, in addition, however* italics for emphasis quotation marks for special uses of words	viewpoint
6 Emergencies and Strange Experiences	other clues to meaning		transition words (effect): *therefore, thus, consequently, as a result, because of this, for this reason*	
7 Health and Illness		understanding an outline: arrangement of topics	colon to introduce lists commas or numbers for items of a series omitted (understood) words	viewpoint
8 Television and the Media		outlines: the place of details		making inferences
9 Friends and Social Life			ellipsis: understanding what is omitted reference words: *this, that, so*	
10 Customs, Celebrations, and Holidays			ellipsis reference	paragraph titles stating the main idea inference
11 Recreation	meaning clues: general to specific	a sentence outline: main ideas	reference	
12 You, the Consumer	general to specific meaning: writing definitions	outlining	the meaning of exaggeration	stating the main ideas stating the viewpoint inference

SUMMARY OF READING SKILLS (continued)
(Blank boxes indicate recycling and review of previous skills)

CHAPTER	PART THREE		PART FOUR
	Building Vocabulary	Study Skills	Scanning for Information
1 School Life	categories of words: people, fields of study, place words in phrases	reading and following instructions	a college catalog: course descriptions
2 Nature	categories of words: places, months, feelings, people, etc. words in phrases	using a dictionary: guide words	weather maps
3 Living to Eat or Eating to Live?	categories words in phrases	increasing reading speed: reading words in phrases	food labels
4 Getting Around the Community	parts of speech: suffixes (nouns, adjectives)	using a dictionary: parts of speech	signs
5 Housing and the Family	categories definitions suffixes (nouns, adjectives, adverbs)	increasing reading speed: reading in phrases	classified ads (housing)
6 Emergencies and Strange Experiences	prefixes	finding reading clues	emergency information (telephone book)
7 Health and Illness	definitions	recognizing paraphrases	medicine labels
8 Television and the Media	prefixes, stems, and suffixes	using the dictionary: definitions (words with more than one meaning)	a TV schedule
9 Friends and Social Life	definitions more suffixes	increasing reading speed: matching synonyms and opposites	newspaper calendar section
10 Customs, Celebrations, and Holidays	related words	using a dictionary: words with more than one meaning	greeting cards
11 Recreation	categories	prediction	a sports roster
12 You, the Consumer	*-ing* and *-ed* adjectives hyphenated words	using a dictionary: word usage	magazine ads

INTERACTIONS I
A Reading Skills Book

1

SCHOOL LIFE

PART ONE

FOREIGN STUDENTS IN THE UNITED STATES AND CANADA

Getting Started

Look at the pictures and talk about them.

1. Name the places, things, and people.
2. Tell stories about the pictures. Where is the place? What kind of place is it? Where are the people from? What do they do?
3. How is this place like your school? How is it different?

2

Preparing to Read

Think about the answers to these questions. The reading selection will answer them.

1. What are foreign students? What are resident aliens? What are nonnative speakers of English?
2. Where do most foreign students go to school?
3. Where do most foreign students come from?
4. What fields of study are popular with foreign students?

3

Glancing at Vocabulary (optional)

Here are some vocabulary items from the reading selection. You can learn them now or come back to them later.

Nouns			Adjectives	Expressions
college	refugee	province	popular	nonnative
university	citizen	oil	foreign	speaker
visa	language	country	practical	nonresident
immigrant	state	fact	important	resident alien
				field of study

Read the following selection quickly. Then answer the questions after the reading.

Foreign Students in the United States and Canada

A   There are many nonnative speakers of English at colleges and universities in the United States and Canada. Nonnatives are usually foreign students or resident aliens. Foreign students in the United States are nonresidents with F or J visas. Resident aliens are immigrants or refugees. In addition, some U.S. and Canadian citizens are nonnative speakers. They do not speak English as their first language.

B   California is the state with the most foreign students. Texas and New York are next. Other states with large numbers of foreign students are Massachusetts, Illinois, Michigan, and Pennsylvania. Students from Europe most often attend school in the northeastern or northwestern states, and students from Asia usually go to school in the midwestern and western states. Latin Americans most often study in the South and Southwest, and Africans usually attend school in the Midwest and South. In Canada, many nonnative speakers study in Quebec and speak French. Some go to school in the provinces of Ontario, Nova Scotia, British Columbia, and Alberta.

C   Engineering is the most popular field of study for visa students. Many study management and business. Most foreign students major in practical subjects.

D   Many visa students in the United States come from the Middle East and Asia, and many are from oil countries. Iran, Taiwan, Nigeria, Japan, Hong Kong, Venezuela, Saudi Arabia, China, India, and Thailand send large numbers of students to the United States. Foreign students in Canada often come from Hong Kong, Malaysia, and the United Kingdom.

E   Visa students are only a small part of the many nonnative speakers at American colleges and universities. But the facts show that nonnatives are very important in American higher education.

Getting the Main Ideas

Write T (true) or F (false) on the lines.

1. _F_   All nonnative speakers of English at American colleges and universities are foreign visa students.

2. _____   All of the facts in this reading selection are about foreign students. They are not about immigrants and refugees.

3. _____   California, Texas, and New York do not have many foreign students.

4. _____   Many nonnative speakers go to school in Ontario and Quebec, Canada.

5. _____   Most visa students study practical subjects.

6. _____   Most foreign students come from Europe.

Guessing Meanings from Context

> You do not need to look up the meanings of all new words in a dictionary. You can guess the meanings of many words from the context.
>
> Sometimes a sentence gives the meaning of a new vocabulary item. The meaning sometimes follows the verb *be*.

Example: The context is the words around the new items.
(What does *context* mean? It means "the words around the new items.")

A. Write the meanings of the underlined words in the following sentences on the lines.

1. Foreign students are nonresidents with F or J visas.
   nonresidents with F or J visas

2. Resident aliens are immigrants or refugees.
   _____

3. Other states with large numbers of foreign students are Massachusetts and Illinois.
   _____

> Sometimes the meaning of a new item is in another sentence or another part of a sentence.
>
> *Example:*   Iran, Venezuela, and other oil countries send many students to the United States. (What are Iran and Venezuela? They are countries with a lot of oil.)

B. Find the meanings of the underlined words in the following sentences. Write them on the lines.

1. Students from Europe most often <u>attend</u> school in the northeastern and northwestern states, and students from Asia usually go to school in the Midwest.

   go to
   _____

2. Many foreign students study management and business. Most <u>major in</u> practical subjects.

   _____

3. Visa students are only a small part of the many nonnative speakers at colleges and universities. But the facts show that nonnatives are very important in American <u>higher education</u>.

   _____

Recognizing Reading Structure

Paragraphs divide reading material into topics. In the reading selection, there is a capital letter next to each of the five paragraphs. One paragraph is usually about one topic.

In this exercise, match each paragraph with its topic. Write the correct letter on the line.

1. _*D*_____   Home countries of foreign students in the United States.

2. _____   Kinds of nonnative speakers

3. _____   Major subjects of foreign students

4. _____   States and parts of the United States and Canada

5. _____   Conclusion or summary

Understanding Details

Circle the letters of the *two* correct phrases for each blank.

1. Nonnative speakers of English can be _____ .

   (a.) foreign students
   (b.) resident immigrants
   c. U.S. or Canadian citizens with English as a native language

2. Facts on foreign students show that many _____ .

   a. attend school in the states of Nevada, Kansas, and Missouri
   b. from South America study in the southern and southwestern parts of the United States
   c. study practical subjects, like engineering and business

3. Large numbers of foreign students come from _____ .

   a. oil countries
   b. Michigan and Pennsylvania
   c. Taiwan, Hong Kong, and Japan

Now turn back to the "Preparing to Read" section on page 3 and answer the questions.

Discussing the Reading

Talk about your answers to the following questions.

1. Are you a visa student, immigrant, tourist, or U.S. or Canadian citizen?
2. Which facts in the reading selection are true for you? (For example, are you a European student in a northeastern U.S. state?) How is your situation different from the description in the reading?
3. Which facts in the reading selection are true in your experience? (For example, do most of your nonnative friends study engineering?) Which facts surprise you? Why?
4. In your opinion, why do most foreign students come to the United States or Canada? Why do they prefer certain states or parts of the country? Why do they prefer practical fields of study?
5. Tell the reasons for your choice of state, school, and major subject.

COLLEGE LIFE IN THE UNITED STATES

Glancing at Vocabulary (optional)

Here are some vocabulary items from the next reading selection. You can learn them now or come back to them later.

Nouns		Verbs	Adjectives	Expressions
campus	test	lead	undergraduate	take notes
professor	textbook	discuss	graduate	teaching
lecture	atmosphere	follow	formal	assistants
discussion	style	offer	informal	midterm
seminar	facility	grade	available	exam(ination)
instructor	counselor		individual	final exam(ination)
classmate	tutor			course outline
assignment	recreation			learning center
homework	service			
quiz				

Skimming for Main Ideas

A paragraph usually tells about one topic. Often one sentence is the "topic sentence." It tells the topic and the main idea of the paragraph. It includes the ideas of the other sentences. The other sentences give details of the main idea.

Example: There are several different kinds of classes on college and university campuses. Professors usually teach large undergraduate classes. They give formal lectures. Students have to listen and take notes. Then teaching assistants (T.A.s) lead discussion groups. In graduate seminars, small groups of students discuss their ideas with their instructor and classmates.

"There are several different kinds of classes on college and university campuses" is the topic sentence of the paragraph. The topic is "kinds of classes." The main idea is "There are several different kinds of classes."

Read the following paragraphs quickly. Then underline the main idea of each paragraph. Remember that the topic sentence is not always the first sentence.

College Life in the United States

A   Instructors at American colleges and universities use many different teaching methods. Some instructors give assignments every day. They grade homework. Students in their classes have to take many quizzes, a midterm exam, and a final exam. Other instructors give only writing assignments. Some teachers always follow a course outline and usually use the textbook. Others send students to the library for assignments.

B   The atmosphere in some classrooms is very formal. Students call their instructors "Professor Smith," "Mrs. Jones," and so on. Some teachers wear business clothes and give lectures. Other classrooms have an informal atmosphere. Students and teachers discuss their ideas. Instructors dress informally, and students call them by their first names. American teachers are not alike in their teaching styles.

C   At most American colleges and universities, facilities for learning and recreation are available to students. Students can often use typewriters, tape recorders, video machines, and computers at libraries and learning centers. They can buy books, notebooks, and other things at campus stores. They can get advice on their problems from counselors and individual help with their classes from tutors. Students can relax and have fun on campus, too. Some schools have swimming pools and tennis courts. Most have snack bars or cafeterias.

Discussing the Reading

Talk about your answers to the following questions.

1. Are any of your classes lectures, discussions, or seminars? What kinds of classes do you prefer? Why?
2. Do you want to have homework and quizzes? Why or why not?
3. Describe the teaching style of your instructors. What style do you prefer? Why?
4. What campus facilities and services do you use? Where are they located?

PART THREE

BUILDING VOCABULARY; STUDY SKILLS

A. Write $\mathscr{p}$ on the lines before the <u>people</u>. Write st before the <u>fields of study</u>. Write pl before the <u>places</u>.

1. ____ immigrant	9. ____ engineering	18. ____ university
2. ____ business	10. ____ campus	19. ____ management
3. ____ library	11. ____ refugee	20. ____ state
4. ____ cafeteria	12. ____ country	21. ____ nonresident
5. ____ citizen	13. ____ instructor	22. ____ tennis court
6. ____ Texas	14. ____ the Midwest	23. ____ Canada
7. ____ undergraduate student	15. ____ counselor	24. ____ teaching assistant
8. ____ Malaysia	16. ____ tutor	25. ____ Ontario
	17. ____ French	

B. Match the parts of the phrase. Write the letter on the line.

1. ____ nonnative		a. recorder
2. ____ a snack		b. counselors
3. ____ a midterm		c. speakers
4. ____ a tape		d. pool
5. ____ student		e. bar
6. ____ a swimming		f. exam

        *   *   *

7. ____ a native		g. of study
8. ____ the northwestern		h. machine
9. ____ a field		i. education
10. ____ higher		j. atmosphere
11. ____ a video		k. language
12. ____ an informal		l. states

Study Skill: Reading and Following Instructions

Textbooks, quizzes, and exams often use special words in their instructions. Follow the instructions and the words. Pay special attention to the verbs.

Which of the following words are examples of which instructions? Match the instructions and the words. Write the words on the lines.

1. Circle the word. *education*   ~~college~~   camp*u*s

2. Underline the word. _____   vo~~cabu~~la~~r~~y   *4* visa

3. Cross out the word. _____   resident   (education)

4. Copy the word. _____   academ *ic* _____✓_____ help

5. Count the words.

   Write the number. _____   fact, oil, state *3*

   your *field* _____ of study

6. Fill in the blank. _____   major *major*

7. Complete the word. _____   country *countries*

8. Divide the word with lines. _____   final↘   ↗student

9. Change the word.   graduate↗ ↘exam

   Write the plural. _____   a _____ assignment

10. Match the words.   a. grade
                                          (b.) homework
    Draw lines. _____   c. facility

11. Cross out the mistake.

    Correct the word. _____

12. Choose the correct word.

    Circle the letter. _____

13. Number the word. _____

14. Put a check by the word. _____

PART FOUR

SCANNING FOR INFORMATION

Sometimes you need to look for information quickly (*scan*). Scanning is *not* careful reading.

Work in small groups. Look at the course descriptions in a college course catalog. Read the questions on pages 13–14. Find the information quickly. Write the answers on the lines. The first group with the correct answers is the winner.

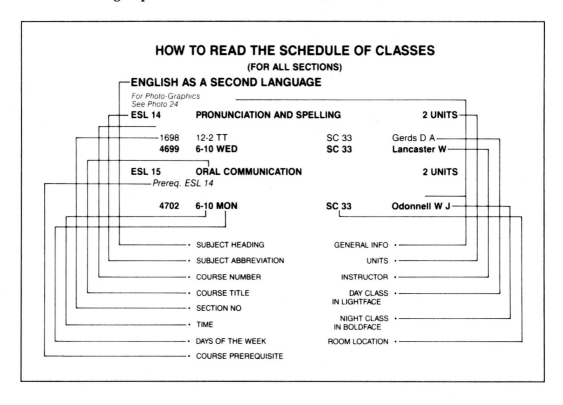

ESL-DEVELOPMENT OF ENGLISH SKILLS

Courses Below Open to Students in English Placement Groups A, B, or C. Make Appointment For Placement Test When Applying For Admission or Anytime in the LRC Before Enrolling.

ESL 11 BASIC ENGLISH 6 UNITS

1711	8-10 MWF	ESL 105	Kenyon A O
1712	8-10:50 TT	ESL 105	Harris J A
1713	10-12 MWF	ESL 105	Jensen L S
4714	**7-10 TT**	**ESL 105**	**Kim H E**

ESL 14 PRONUNCIATION AND SPELLING 2 UNITS

Teaches Non-Native English Speakers Pronunciation and Spelling. Material Fee of $2.00 Is

| 1715 | 8 MWF | ESL 123 | Harris J A |
| 1716 | 8-9:15 TT | ESL 125 | Ruskin J L |

ESL 15 ORAL COMMUNICATION 2 UNITS

Teaches Advanced Non-Native English Speakers How to Express Opinions and Ideas More Clearly and Fluently. Students Participate in Small Groups.

1717	12 MWF	ESL 123	Fonseca M L
1718	1-2:15 TT	ESL 103	Hartnett D D
4719	**7-10 MON**	**LA 136**	**Gough J W**

ESL 16B USING VERB TENSES 1 UNIT

Recommended For Students Who Have Difficulty With Verb Tenses.

4723	7-10 PM, WED	SC 251	Gough J W
	Above Section 4723 Meets For Nine Weeks and Starts Sept. 14		
1722	8 MWF	ESL 125	Fonseca J L

1. What is the subject heading (department) for this section of the catalog? _____

2. How many ESL courses are there? ____

3. What do students learn about in ESL 14? _____

4. How many different instructors teach ESL 16B? ____

    a. What are the instructors' last names? _____

    b. What are the instructors' initials? _____

5. How many sections of ESL 11 are there? _____

    a. How many sections meet in the morning? _____

    b. At what time does the evening section meet? _____

    c. How many days a week does it meet? _____

6. How many classes meet in classrooms *not* in the ESL building? _____

7. Where does the ESL 16B class meet at 8:00 in the morning? _____

8. What course teaches how to express ideas and opinions? _____

9. Which course gives more college credit—ESL 11 or ESL 15? _____

10. Which course or courses interests you? Why? _____

Going Beyond the Text

Bring to class reading material about college life. Some examples are catalogs, course schedules, school newspapers, and orientation information. Share them with the class. Discuss the important information and learn new vocabulary.

PART FIVE

PERSONAL STORIES

Follow these steps for the stories:

1. Read them quickly and tell the main ideas.
2. Answer your instructor's questions about the stories, or ask and answer questions of your own.
3. Tell your opinions of the ideas in the stories.
4. Tell or write your own story about education or college life.

Educational Systems

A   I can't stand American college life. I like my teachers and classmates, but I don't like the system of daily classes, assignments, and tests. In my country, students have more freedom and less structure. They don't have to attend lectures or seminars every day. They don't do homework or have quizzes in their courses. They just have to get a certificate of completion for a certain number of courses. The certificate is proof of attendance. After three to five years of attendance, they take final exams. If they pass these important tests, they get a university degree.

B   I don't like the teaching style in American college classes. My instructors and classmates are nice, but I can't stand the system of undergraduate education at the university. In my country, students have more structure and less freedom. They have to attend lectures every day and do homework assignments in their textbooks. The professor gives them outlines of the important facts. They have a test and get a grade in every course every week. The questions are multiple choice or fill-in-the-blank, and students just have to choose the correct answer. But in the United States, students take notes, ask questions, and discuss their ideas. I don't like to do those things.

2

NATURE

THE POWERFUL INFLUENCE OF WEATHER

Getting Started

Look at the pictures and talk about them.

1. Describe the people. What are they wearing? What are they carrying? Why?
2. Describe the kinds of weather. Which kind do you like best? Why?

16

Preparing to Read

Think about the answers to these questions. (The reading selection will answer them.)

1. How does the weather affect people's health, intelligence, and feelings?
2. What kinds of weather have an influence on people?
3. What is the "perfect weather"?

Glancing at Vocabulary (optional)

Here are some vocabulary items from the reading selection. You can learn them now or come back to them later.

Nouns		Verbs	Adjectives	Expressions
weather	storm	relax	powerful	below average
effect	temperature	increase	strong	air pressure
health	degree (°)	grow	perfect	on the other hand
intelligence	humidity			
percent (%)	cause			
feeling				

Read the following selection quickly. Then answer the questions after the reading.

The Powerful Influence of Weather

A   Weather has a powerful effect on people. It influences health, intelligence, and feelings.

B   In August, it is very hot and wet in the southern part of the United States. Southerners have heart attacks and other kinds of health problems during this month. In the Northeast and the Middle West, it is very hot at some times and very cold at other times. People in these states tend to have heart attacks after the weather changes in February or March.

C   The weather can also influence intelligence. For example, in a 1938 study by scientists, the IQ scores of a group of undergraduate college students were very high during a hurricane, but after the storm, their scores were 10 percent (%) below average. Hurricanes can increase intelligence. Very hot weather, on the other hand, can lower it. Students in many of the United States often do badly on exams in the hot months of the year (July and August).

D   Weather also has a strong influence on people's feelings. Winter may be a bad time for thin people. They usually feel cold during these months. They might feel depressed during cold weather. In hot summer weather, on the other hand, fat people may feel unhappy. At about 65°F, people become stronger.

E   Low air pressure relaxes people. It increases sexual feelings. It also increases forgetfulness. People leave more packages and umbrellas on buses and in stores on low-pressure days. There is a "perfect weather" for work and health. People feel best at a temperature of about 64°F with 65 percent humidity (moisture in the air).

F   Are you feeling sick, sad, tired, forgetful, or very intelligent today? The weather may be the cause.

Getting the Main Ideas

Write T (true) or F (false) on the lines.

1. _____ The weather influences people's health and feelings.

2. _____ There are the same number of heart attacks in every part of the United States in every month of the year.

3. _____ Intelligence (IQ) never changes.

4. _____ Hot and cold weather affect all people the same way.

5. _____ Some weather influences are temperature, storms, and air pressure.

6. _____ There is a perfect kind of weather for peoples' work and health.

Guessing Meaning from Context

Sometimes a sentence gives the meaning of a new vocabulary item. The meaning or an explanation is sometimes in parentheses (   ), in another sentence, or in another sentence part.

Example: The *IQ scores* (measure of intelligence) of a group of undergraduate college students were very high during a hurricane or other kind of storm. (What are "IQ scores"? They are "measures of intelligence." What is a "hurricane"? It is a kind of storm.)

Write the meanings of the underlined words in the following sentences on the lines.

1. Students often do badly on exams in the hot months of the year (July and August).

   the hot months of the year

2. At about 65°F (degrees Fahrenheit), people become stronger.

   _____

3. In "perfect weather" the humidity (moisture in the air) is about 65 percent.

   _____

4. Weather has a powerful effect on people. It also has a strong influence on people's feelings.

   _____

5. Thin people might feel depressed during cold weather. Fat people, on the other hand, may feel unhappy in hot summer months.

   _____

Recognizing Reading Structure

A. In the reading selection, there is a letter next to each of the six paragraphs. In this exercise, match each paragraph with its topic. Write the correct letter on the line.

1. _____   The influence of weather on people's feelings

2. _____   The effect of air pressure on people

3. _____   The effects of heat, cold, and weather changes on people's health

4. _____   Conclusion or summary

5. _____   Introduction

6. _____   The influence of weather on intelligence

> A reading may express one main idea. The main idea includes the topics and ideas of all the paragraphs in the reading. The main idea may be in a topic sentence.

B. Circle the number of the *one* main idea of the reading.

1. Low air pressure relaxes people.
2. Weather has a strong effect on people.
3. After the storm, people's scores were 10 percent below average.
4. There is a "perfect weather" for work and health.

Understanding Details

Which *two* phrases are correct for each blank, according to the reading selection? Circle the letters.

1. _____ may have a bad effect on health.

    a. hot, wet weather   c. weather changes
    b. perfect weather   d. high intelligence

2. Intelligence may increase because of _____ .

    a. storms   c. a hurricane
    b. very hot weather   d. low air pressure

3. Low air pressure _____ .

    a. depresses fat people   c. increases forgetfulness
    b. relaxes people   d. causes heart attacks

4. In "perfect" weather of 64°F, _____ .

    a. people are very forgetful   c. people work well
    b. thin people feel cold   d. people are in better health

Now turn back to the "Preparing to Read" section on page 17 and answer the questions.

Discussing the Reading

Talk about your answers to the following questions.

1. How is the weather in your country? What are the seasons? How and when do they change?
2. Which facts in the reading are true for you? (For example, do you feel more intelligent during storms?)
3. Do you believe that the weather affects health and feelings? Why or why not?
4. What kind of weather is perfect for you? Why?

PART TWO

CAMPING

Glancing at Vocabulary (optional)

Here are some vocabulary items from the next reading selection. You can learn them now or come back to them later.

Nouns	Verbs
camping	protect
camper	cook
equipment	set up
tent	
wind	Adjectives
park	magnificent
forest	spectacular
scenery	crowded
wilderness	national
hiking	
rain	Adverb
insect	fortunately
backpack	
campground	
fishing	
hunting	
wildlife	
solitude	

Skimming for Main Ideas

Read each of the following three paragraphs quickly. Then underline the main idea of each paragraph. (Remember that it is not always the first sentence.)

Camping

A   Camping is a popular form of recreation in the United States and Canada. For camping, you need equipment. In this picture, two campers are setting up an umbrella tent. The tent will protect them from the cold, the wind and the rain, and insects. Other people are cooking on a small gas stove. A camping stove is safe and easy. There are two hikers carrying backpacks. Their sleeping bags are light but warm.

B   There is magnificent scenery in the national parks and forests of the United States and Canada. Yellowstone National Park in Wyoming, for example, offers spectacular geysers. Utah's Arches National Monument has beautiful red rock formations. At Alaska's Glacier Bay, there are magnificent ice fields.

C   The campgrounds in the popular national parks and forests are often very crowded, especially in spring and summer. Fortunately, wilderness areas offer many advantages to hikers and campers. In these parts of the national park or forest systems, there are no roads, no campgrounds, and no restrooms or showers, but there *is* great hiking, swimming, fishing, and hunting. There is also magnificent scenery (hills, mountains, rivers, and waterfalls, lakes, forests, and meadows). And there are not many people enjoying the trees and flowers, the wildlife, and the solitude of the wilderness.

Discussing the Reading

Talk about your answers to the following questions.

1. Do you like camping and hiking? Why or why not?
2. Where do you go camping or hiking? What equipment do you take?
3. What do you do on your camping trips or hikes? What do you see?

PART THREE

BUILDING VOCABULARY; STUDY SKILLS

A. One word does not belong in each of the following groups. Cross out the word. Explain your decisions.

1. hot cold ~~best~~ wet	3. sick tired sad best	5. hurricane intelligence storm rain	7. February spring summer winter	9. July August Northeast March
2. insect stove backpack tent	4. park relax forest field	6. restroom solitude campground shower	8. mountain meadow wildlife lake	10. hiking scenery fishing hunting

B. Follow the directions for each of the following items.

1. Circle the kinds of weather:

   wind   southern   attack   rain   humidity   score

2. Draw a box around the places:

   the Middle West   umbrella   cause   national park   hill

3. Check the living things:

   changes   trees   flowers   wildlife   areas   rocks

4. Cross out the kinds of scenery:

   river   waterfall   meadow   forest   campfire   counselor

C. Can the words in each of the following pairs together make a phrase? Write *yes* or *no* on the lines.

1. *yes*   cold–weather
2. *no*   native–especially
3. _____   below–average
4. _____   low–pressure
5. _____   crowded–campsite

6. _____   strong–influence
7. _____   practical–fortunately
8. _____   attend–forgetful
9. _____   magnificent–scenery
10. _____   national–parks

Study Skill: Using a Dictionary (Guide Words)

You can often guess the meaning of new words from the context. Sometimes, however, you may want to use your dictionary for other purposes. With a dictionary, you can check spelling and pronunciation; you can find out parts of speech; you can increase your vocabulary.

All dictionaries have "guide words" at the top of each page. These words help you find entries quickly. The word on the left is the first entry on the page; the word on the right is the last entry on the page.

A. If possible, everyone in the class uses the same kind of dictionary for this exercise. Work quickly. The first student with the correct answers is the winner. Write the guide words for these pages.

	FIRST WORD	LAST WORD
1. page 215:		
2. page 134:		
3. page 45:		
4. page 178:		
5. page 265:		

B. Write guide words from your dictionary on the following lines. Then work with a partner. Exchange books. Each student writes the page numbers for each pair of words. Work quickly. The first student with the correct answers is the winner.

1. page ____   _____   _____

2. page ____   _____   _____

3. page ____   _____   _____

4. page ____   _____   _____

5. page ____   _____   _____

C. Work quickly. The first student with the correct answers is the winner. Write the page numbers and the guide words from your dictionary for each of the following entries:

1. tired: page ____   _____   _____

2. tutor: page ____   _____   _____

3. scientist: page ____   _____   _____

4. southern: page ____   _____   _____

5. pressure: page ____   _____   _____

PART FOUR

SCANNING FOR INFORMATION

Work in small groups. Look at the weather report in the newspaper. Pretend it is for today's weather. Read the questions on page 26. Find the information quickly. Write the answers on the lines.

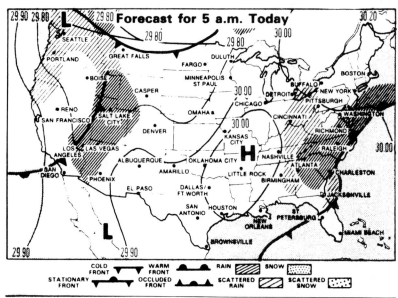

City Forecasts

LOS ANGELES: Today—cloudy during morning hours; becoming partly cloudy in afternoon; highs near 80. Tonight—lows 66.

Forecast for 5 a.m. Today

COLD FRONT   WARM FRONT   RAIN   SNOW

STATIONARY FRONT   OCCLUDED FRONT   SCATTERED RAIN   SCATTERED SNOW

Global Report

Gathered by Associated Press for Friday, local time, and by the National Weather Service:

City	Cond.	Hi/Lo	City	Cond.	Hi/Lo	City	Cond.	Hi/Lo
Acapulco	Rain	79/75	Guadalajara	Clear	84/50	Nicosia	Clear	91/63
Amsterdam	Cloudy	63/50	Havana	Cloudy	84/73	Oslo	Cloudy	52/50
Athens	Clear	86/66	Helsinki	Clear	55/36	Paris	Cloudy	70/59
Bangkok	Clear	88/81	Hong Kong	Rain	79/77	Peking	Cloudy	79/55
Barbados	Cloudy	85/75	Jerusalem	Clear	82/61	Rio de Janeiro	Cloudy	82/59
Beirut	Clear	75/64	Johannesburg	Clear	73/52	Rome	Clear	79/64
Belgrade	Clear	81/57	Kiev	Rain	73/54	Sao Paulo	Cloudy	72/57
Berlin	Clear	64/48	Kingston	Fair	91/79	Seoul	Clear	82/55
Bogota	Cloudy	64/45	Lima	Cloudy	70/59	Singapore	Cloudy	90/79
Brussels	Rain	64/50	Lisbon	Cloudy	68/59	Stockholm	Clear	61/32
Buenos Aires	Clear	68/61	London	Cloudy	63/55	Sydney	Clear	75/50
Cairo	Clear	90/64	Madrid	Cloudy	72/50	Taipei	Clear	86/72
Calgary		No report	Manila	Clear	86/73	Tel Aviv	Clear	82/69
Caracas	Cloudy	82/64	Mazatlan	Ptcldy	99/73	Tokyo	Rain	72/64
Copenhagen	Cloudy	63/53	Mexico City	Cloudy	70/53	Toronto	Rain	61/50
Dublin	Rain	57/48	Montreal	Cloudy	68/48	Vancouver	Rain	63/50
Edmonton		No report	Moscow	Clear	68/55	Veracruz	Cloudy	88/72
Frankfurt	Cloudy	70/48	Nassau	Cloudy	90/73	Vienna	Cloudy	63/54
Geneva	Cloudy	55/39	New Delhi	Clear	91/72	Winnipeg		No report

1. What city of the United States is this newspaper from? How do you know? ____

    _____

2. Are the temperatures in Fahrenheit or Centigrade (Celsius)? _____

3. Is it cloudy or sunny in Los Angeles today? _____

4. What will the highest temperature in Los Angeles be? _____

5. What do the dark lines on the map of the United States mean? _____

6. Where is it raining in the United States today? _____

    _____

7. Where is it snowing? _____

8. What season is it probably? How do you know? _____

    _____

9. What is a "global report"? _____

10. Is it raining today in Acapulco, Mexico? _____

11. What is today's high temperature in Berlin, Germany? _____

12. In which Asian cities is it sunny today? _____

    _____

13. Which city has the highest temperature today? _____

14. What kind of weather does your native city probably have today? _____

    _____

Going Beyond the Text

Bring to class newspaper weather reports. Listen to weather reports on the radio and TV. Summarize the information and discuss new vocabulary.

Collect brochures about national parks and forests. Look at the pictures and discuss the information.

PART FIVE

PERSONAL STORIES

Follow these steps for the story:

1. Read it quickly and tell the main ideas.
2. Answer your instructor's questions about the story, or ask and answer questions of your own.
3. Tell your opinions of the ideas in the story.
4. Tell or write your own story about travel or nature.

Traveling and Nature

It's hot and humid in my city in the summer. The weather has a strong influence on my feelings and health, and I often feel depressed in July and August. I feel best at a temperature under eighty degrees with low humidity, so I want to travel to the Northwest. Fortunately, my best friend and I can drive. We'll see magnificent scenery and relax. We may stay at campgrounds in some national parks and forests.

I have many brochures and other travel information from a government office.* I especially like to look at picture books of the United States and Canada at the school or public library. We may also get ideas from travel magazines and the travel section of the newspaper. My friend belongs to "Triple A" (the American Automobile Association), too. The AAA will give him maps and tourbooks. We can plan our trip with their help.

What will we take with us on our trip? It's a small car, and we have to pack some camping equipment. We'll take only the necessary clothing. Some other important items are a Swiss army knife (with scissors, a bottle opener, and other things), an ice chest, a small medical kit, and of course a camera.

My friend and I are planning our trip now, but it isn't easy. He wants to see the magnificent ice fields of Alaska's Glacier Bay, but I'm thinking about the spectacular geysers of Yellowstone National Park in Wyoming. He's talking about the islands of northwestern Canada, but I want to spend time in the Grand Teton Mountains of Wyoming. We have two weeks for a trip.

---

*For free travel information, you can write the U.S. Travel and Tour Administration, Department of Commerce, 14th and Constitution Avenue Northwest, Washington, DC 20230.

3

LIVING TO EAT OR EATING TO LIVE?

PART ONE

OUR CHANGING DIET

Getting Started

Look at the pictures and talk about them.

1. Where are the people and what are they doing?
2. How are these scenes like scenes in your country? How are they different?
3. Which scene or scenes do you prefer? Why?

28

Preparing to Read

Think about the answers to these questions. (The reading selection will answer them.)

1. What does the typical American or Canadian usually eat?
2. What is wrong with the typical North American diet?
3. How are people changing their eating habits?
4. What kinds of food will we eat in the future?

Glancing at Vocabulary (optional)

Here are some vocabulary items from the reading selection. You can learn them now or come back to them later.

Nouns	Verbs	Adjectives	Expression
diet	consist (of)	typical	and so on
vitamins	contain	frozen	
fat	include	canned	
value	provide	healthful	
habit			
health			
protein			

Read the following selection quickly. Then answer the questions after the reading.

Our Changing Diet

A   What does the typical American or Canadian usually eat? Most people think that the typical North American diet consists of fast foods—hamburgers and french fries. It also includes convenience foods, usually frozen or canned, "junk food" without much food value—candy, potato chips, cereal with lots of sugar but no vitamins—and so on. This diet is very high in sugar, salt, fat, and cholesterol, and the choice of food does not provide much good nutrition.

B   However, eating habits are changing. North Americans are becoming more interested in good health, and nutrition is an important part of health. People are eating less red meat and fewer eggs, and they are eating more chicken and fish. They know that chicken and fish are better for their health than meat or eggs because these foods do not contain much fat or cholesterol. Some foods might cause health problems, and people want to stay away from them.

C   For health reasons, many people are also buying more fresh vegetables. They may eat them without cooking them first, or they might cook them quickly in very little water because they want to keep the vitamins.

D   The "typical" North American diet now includes food from many different countries. More ethnic restaurants are opening in big cities in the United States and Canada. Foods from Japan, Thailand, Mexico, West Africa, China, and India are very popular. At lunchtime, many people go to ethnic fast-food places for a Mexican taco, Middle Eastern falafel, or Philippine lumpia.

E How are we going to eat in the future? We will probably continue to eat more fish and vegetables and less meat. We will still buy convenience foods, but frozen foods will be better for our health, and canned foods will have less salt and sugar. Our "junk food" in the future is not really going to be "junk" at all, because instead of candy bars we are going to eat "nutrition bars" with a lot of vitamins and protein. In the future, our diet will probably be even more interesting and healthful than it is now.

Getting the Main Ideas

Write T (true) or F (false) on the lines.

1. _____ All North Americans eat only fast foods, convenience foods, and "junk foods" with a lot of sugar, salt, and fat.

2. _____ People today are becoming more interested in good nutrition and more healthful cooking methods.

3. _____ Foods from other countries are not very popular among North Americans.

4. _____ In the future, people will probably continue to eat more healthful foods.

Guessing Meaning from Context

Sometimes a sentence gives the meaning of a new vocabulary item. Punctuation may give clues to the meaning. A meaning or an explanation is sometimes in parentheses ( ), after a dash (—), or after a comma (,). Sometimes the meaning is in another sentence or sentence part.

Examples: Mexican *tacos* (meat and vegetables in *tortillas*—a flat kind of Mexican bread) are popular in the southwestern part of the United States. People eat them with *hot sauce,* a sauce of tomatoes and spicy chili peppers.

What are tortillas? They are a flat kind of Mexican bread. What are tacos? They are tortillas with meat and vegetables in them. What is hot sauce? It is a sauce of tomatoes and spicy chili peppers.

Write the meanings of the underlined words in the following sentences on the lines.

1. Most people think that the typical North American diet consists of <u>fast foods</u> (hamburgers and french fries). It also includes <u>convenience foods</u>, usually frozen or canned, and "<u>junk food</u>"—candy, potato chips, cereal with lots of sugar but no vitamins, and so on.

   fast foods: *hamburgers and french fries*

   convenience foods: _____

   junk food: _____

2. People are eating more chicken and fish—foods without much fat or <u>cholesterol</u> (a kind of fat).

   cholesterol: _____

3. The "typical" North American diet now includes food from many different countries—"<u>ethnic</u>" foods.

   ethnic: _____

4. The typical American <u>diet</u> includes convenience foods and junk food without much food value. This <u>choice of food</u> is very high in sugar, salt, and fat, but it does not provide much good <u>nutrition</u>.

   diet: _____

   nutrition: _____

5. For health reasons, many people are also buying more <u>raw</u> vegetables. They may eat the vegetables uncooked, or they might cook them quickly in very little water.

   raw: _____

Recognizing Reading Structure

A. In the reading selection, there is a capital letter next to each of the five paragraphs. In this exercise, match each paragraph with its topic. Write the correct letter on the line.

1. _____ Ideas about the "typical" North American diet of the past

2. _____ Ideas about food and eating habits in the future

3. _____ Vegetables and ways to eat them

4. _____ Ethnic foods in the North American diet

5. _____ How and why people are changing their eating habits

B. Circle the number of the *one* main idea of the reading.

1. The "typical" North American diet now includes food from many different countries.
2. For health reasons, many people are also buying more raw vegetables.
3. Our "junk food" in the future is not really going to be "junk" at all.
4. North Americans are becoming more interested in good health, and nutrition is an important part of health.

Understanding Details

Connecting words (*and, but, or, because,* and so on) often provide clues to the meaning of sentences and paragraphs.

Examples: For health reasons, we will continue to eat more fish, *and* we may eat less meat. (We will eat more fish for health reasons. We will eat less meat for health reasons. Fish is more healthful than meat.)

We are still going to eat candy bars, *but* they will have a lot of vitamins and protein. (Candy bars do not contain many vitamins or much protein. By contrast, in the future they will contain vitamins and protein.)

At lunchtime, people may eat in a Chinese restaurant, *or* they might go to a fast-food place for a Mexican taco. (People might choose between a Chinese restaurant or a Mexican fast-food place.)

People do not want to eat some foods *because* they might cause health problems. (Why don't people want to eat some foods? They might cause health problems.)

Find the answers to these questions in the reading selection on pages 30–31. Write them on the lines.

1. What foods are North Americans eating more for better nutrition?

    _____

2. What foods are they eating less?

    _____

3. Why do people cook vegetables quickly in very little water?

    _____

4. What kinds of ethnic foods do North Americans often eat?

    _____

5. How will convenience foods change in the future?

    _____

6. Why will "junk food" be more healthful?

    _____

Now turn back to the "Preparing to Read" section on page 29 and answer the questions.

Discussing the Reading

Talk about your answers to the following questions.

1. What was your idea of the typical American diet before your arrival in the United States or Canada? Are your ideas changing?
2. What do you think about fast foods, convenience foods, and junk food? Do you have these foods in your country?
3. Can you give three or four reasons for the changes in the American diet?
4. Do you often go to ethnic restaurants? If so, what kinds of restaurants? If not, why not?
5. What kind of food do you most often eat? Are you trying any new foods?

PART TWO

FOOD PERSONALITIES

Glancing at Vocabulary (optional)

Here are some vocabulary items from the next reading section. You can learn them now or come back to them later.

Nouns	Adjectives	Expressions
personality	gourmet	human being
study	similar	astrological sign
expression	creative	have in common
	competitive	
Verbs	common	
express	born	
agree	spicy	

Skimming for Main Ideas

Read the following paragraphs quickly. Then underline the main idea of each paragraph.

Food Personalities

A   People express their personalities in their clothes, their cars, and their homes. Because we might choose certain foods to "tell" people something about us, our diets can also be an expression of our personalities. For example, some people eat mainly gourmet foods, such as caviar and lobster, and they eat only in expensive restaurants (never in cafeterias or snack bars). They might want to "tell" the world that they know about the "better things in life."

B   Human beings can eat many different kinds of food, but some people choose not to eat meat. Vegetarians often have more in common than just their diet. Their personalities might be similar, too. For example, vegetarians in the United States may be creative people, and they might not enjoy competitive sports or jobs. They worry about the health of the world, and they probably don't believe in war.

C   Some people eat mostly "fast food." One study shows that many fast-food eaters have a lot in common with one another, but they are very different from vegetarians. They are competitive and good at business. They are also usually in a hurry. Many fast-food eaters might not agree with this description of their personalities, but it is a common picture of them.

D Some people also believe that people of the same astrological sign have similar food personalities. Arians (born under the sign of Aries, between March 21 and April 19) usually like spicy food, with a lot of onions and pepper. People with the sign of Taurus (April 20 to May 20) prefer healthful fruits and vegetables, but they often eat too much. Sagittarians (November 22 to December 21) like ethnic foods from many different countries. Aquarians (January 20 to February 18) can eat as much meat and fish as they want, but sugar and cholesterol are sometimes problems for them.

Discussing the Reading

Talk about your answers to the following questions.

1. What kind of food do you eat most often? Why? Does this kind of food express your personality?
2. Do you know any gourmet eaters? Vegetarians? Fast-food eaters? In your opinion, what kind of people are they?
3. Do you believe the information in this reading? Why or why not?

PART THREE

BUILDING VOCABULARY; STUDY SKILLS

A. Write *f* on the lines before the kind of *food*. Write *e* before the *elements* (parts) of food. Write *pl* before the food *places*.

1. ____ restaurant	7. ____ protein	12. ____ candy
2. ____ vitamins	8. ____ red meat	13. ____ vegetables
3. ____ fruit	9. ____ fat	14. ____ cholesterol
4. ____ cafeteria	10. ____ cereal	15. ____ snack bar
5. ____ chicken	11. ____ caviar	16. ____ fish
6. ____ lobster		

B. Circle the letters of *all* the words that might fit in the blanks.

1. People _____ their personalities in their clothes.

   a. show   b. choose   c. express   d. worry

2. Some people eat mainly _____ food.

   a. meat   b. gourmet   c. fast   d. canned

3. Fast-food eaters _____ vegetarians.

   a. are different from   c. do not agree with
   b. are not similar to   d. are learning

4. You can buy _____ foods at the supermarket.

   a. nutritious   b. canned   c. frozen   d. typical

Study Skill: Increasing Reading Speed

Students usually need to read quickly because they have to read a lot of material. Reading speed is important to students. Also, fast readers usually understand reading material better than slow readers.

Slow readers usually read one word at a time.

Example: People   express   their   personalities   in   their   clothes,   their   cars,   and   their   homes.

Average readers usually read a few words together (short phrases) at a time.

Example: People express   their personalities   in their clothes,   their cars,   and their homes.

Fast readers usually read several words (longer phrases) at a time.

Example: People express their personalities   in their clothes, cars, and homes.

You can improve your reading speed with practice.

A. Read the following sentences in phrases, as shown.

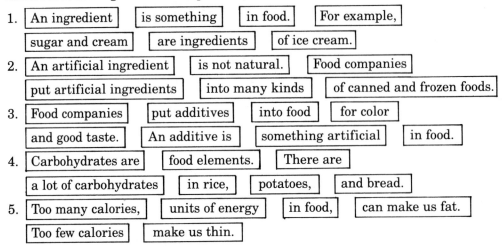

1. [An ingredient] [is something] [in food.] [For example,]
[sugar and cream] [are ingredients] [of ice cream.]

2. [An artificial ingredient] [is not natural.] [Food companies]
[put artificial ingredients] [into many kinds] [of canned and frozen foods.]

3. [Food companies] [put additives] [into food] [for color]
[and good taste.] [An additive is] [something artificial] [in food.]

4. [Carbohydrates are] [food elements.] [There are]
[a lot of carbohydrates] [in rice,] [potatoes,] [and bread.]

5. [Too many calories,] [units of energy] [in food,] [can make us fat.]
[Too few calories] [make us thin.]

A *noun phrase* includes adjectives and other words before or after a noun. A
verb phrase may include noun objects, adjectives, or adverbs in addition to a
verb. A *prepositional phrase* includes an object after a preposition.

Examples:

Noun Phrases	Verb Phrases	Prepositional Phrases
one-half cup	make us fat	in food
too much cholesterol	is not natural	of ice cream
artificial additives	contains calories	with a spoon
units of energy	eat slowly	

B. In the following sentences, which words belong together? Read the sentences in
phrases. (There may be several correct possibilities.) Separate the phrases with
lines.

1. The RDA | —the recommended daily allowance— | is the necessary daily amount |
of a food element | for one person.

2. Half-and-half, a mixture of half cream and half milk, contains fewer calories
than pure cream.

3. White flour in white bread does not have important B vitamins—for example,
folic acid, niacin, and vitamin B12.

4. A *serving of food* is the average amount of that food for one person for one meal. An average serving of half-and-half is one-half cup.

5. Minerals—natural elements in food such as cobalt, copper, magnesium, and zinc—are as necessary to our diets as vitamins.

6. A gram is a unit of weight. It is 1/1000 of a kilogram. A tablespoon is a unit of measure equal to three teaspoons, or one-half fluid ounce.

7. Most cans, bottles, and other food packages have labels. These labels give nutritional information about the food in the packages.

PART FOUR

SCANNING FOR INFORMATION

A. Match the following words on the left-hand side with their meanings on the right-hand side. Write the correct letter on the line. For clues to the words' meanings, review the exercises in Part Three.

1. ____ calories	a.	an artificial ingredient
2. ____ serving	b.	things in food
	c.	not natural
3. ____ gram	d.	units of food energy
4. ____ artificial	e.	elements of food in things like rice, bread, and potatoes
5. ____ label	f.	average amount of a kind of food for one person for one meal
6. ____ minerals		
7. ____ ingredients	g.	the necessary daily amount of a food element for one person
8. ____ carbohydrates	h.	natural element in food, such as copper or zinc
	i.	a unit of weight
9. ____ additive	j.	the paper on a food package with nutritional information
10. ____ RDA		

Note: You can read the ingredients on the packages of many foods. The ingredients are in the order of amount. The greatest amount comes first. Also, the amount of calories, carbohydrates, protein, fat, vitamins, and minerals in the foods are often listed on the package. There is also a list of the RDA of vitamins and minerals.

B. Look at the food labels. Read the following questions and find the information as fast as you can. Write the answers on the lines.

MAYONNAISE

NUTRITION INFORMATION PER SERVING

SERVING SIZE	1 TABLESPOON (14 GRAMS)
SERVINGS PER CONTAINER	16
CALORIES	100
PROTEIN	0 GRAMS
CARBOHYDRATE	0 GRAMS
FAT	11 GRAMS
PERCENT OF CALORIES FROM FAT†	99%
POLYUNSATURATED†	5 GRAMS
SATURATED	2 GRAMS
CHOLESTEROL† (50 MG/100 G)	10 MILLIGRAMS
SODIUM (565 MG/100 G)	80 MILLIGRAMS

PERCENTAGE OF U.S. RECOMMENDED DAILY ALLOWANCES (U.S. RDA)

CONTAINS LESS THAN 2 PERCENT OF THE U.S. RDA OF PROTEIN, VITAMIN A, VITAMIN C, THIAMINE, RIBOFLAVIN, NIACIN, CALCIUM, IRON.

†INFORMATION ON FAT AND CHOLESTEROL CONTENT IS PROVIDED FOR INDIVIDUALS WHO, ON THE ADVICE OF A PHYSICIAN, ARE MODIFYING THEIR TOTAL DIETARY INTAKE OF FAT AND/OR CHOLESTEROL.

INGREDIENTS: SOYBEAN OIL, PARTIALLY HYDROGENATED SOYBEAN OIL, WHOLE EGGS, VINEGAR, WATER, EGG YOLKS, SALT, SUGAR, LEMON JUICE, AND NATURAL FLAVORS. CALCIUM DISODIUM EDTA ADDED TO PROTECT FLAVOR.

BEST FOODS, CPC INTERNATIONAL INC. GENERAL OFFICES, ENGLEWOOD CLIFFS, NJ 07632

The Inter-Society Commission for Heart Disease Resources has recommended that the average daily intake of cholesterol be reduced to less than 300 mg per day. With only 10 mg per tablespoon, Best Foods Real Mayonnaise is low in cholesterol.

CUT GREEN BEANS
NO SALT ADDED

INGREDIENTS: GREEN BEANS, WATER.

NUTRITION INFORMATION — PER 1/2 CUP SERVING
SERVINGS PER CONTAINER — APPROX. 4

CALORIES	20
PROTEIN	1g
CARBOHYDRATE	4g
FAT	0g
SODIUM	LESS THAN 10mg

PERCENTAGE OF U.S. RECOMMENDED DAILY ALLOWANCES (U.S. RDA) PER 1/2 CUP SERVING

VITAMIN A	10
VITAMIN C	6
THIAMINE (VIT. B_1)	2
RIBOFLAVIN (VIT. B_2)	2
CALCIUM	2
IRON	4
PHOSPHORUS	2
MAGNESIUM	2

CONTAINS LESS THAN 2% OF THE U.S. RDA OF PROTEIN AND NIACIN.
©1982 DISTRIBUTED BY DEL MONTE CORPORATION SAN FRANCISCO, CA 94105 — PACKED IN U.S.A.
*WT. OF BEANS (8¾ OZ.) BEFORE ADDITION OF LIQUID NECESSARY FOR PROCESSING.
Net Wt... 16 oz. (1 lb.) 454g   Cups.. Approx. 2
For good nutrition eat a variety of foods.

0   24000 01264

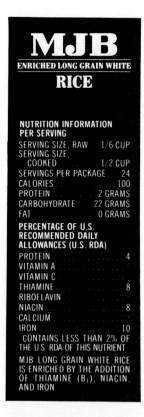

MJB
ENRICHED LONG GRAIN WHITE
RICE

NUTRITION INFORMATION PER SERVING

SERVING SIZE, RAW	1/6 CUP
SERVING SIZE, COOKED	1/2 CUP
SERVINGS PER PACKAGE	24
CALORIES	100
PROTEIN	2 GRAMS
CARBOHYDRATE	22 GRAMS
FAT	0 GRAMS

PERCENTAGE OF U.S. RECOMMENDED DAILY ALLOWANCES (U.S. RDA)

PROTEIN	4
VITAMIN A	
VITAMIN C	
THIAMINE	8
RIBOFLAVIN	
NIACIN	8
CALCIUM	
IRON	10

CONTAINS LESS THAN 2% OF THE U.S. RDA OF THIS NUTRIENT.

MJB LONG GRAIN WHITE RICE IS ENRICHED BY THE ADDITION OF THIAMINE (B_1), NIACIN, AND IRON.

HOMOGENIZED HALF AND HALF

INGREDIENTS: MILK & CREAM.

NUTRITION INFORMATION PER SERVING
Serving Size ..... ONE HALF CUP (4 fl. oz.)
Servings per Container 4
Calories 160   Carbohydrate .5 grams
Protein ... 4 grams   Fat .... 14 grams

PERCENTAGE OF U.S. RECOMMENDED DAILY ALLOWANCES (U.S. RDA)

Protein	10	Vitamin D	4
Vitamin A	8	Vitamin B_6	2
Vitamin C	2	Vitamin B_{12}	6
Thiamine	2	Phosphorus	10
Riboflavin	12	Magnesium	4
Niacin	*	Zinc	2
Calcium	15	Pantothenic	
Iron	*	Acid	2

*Contains less than 2% of the U.S. RDA of these nutrients.

1. What foods do these labels come from? _____

    _____

2. What things are in a can of green beans? (What are the ingredients?) _____

    _____

3. What are the main ingredients of mayonnaise? _____

    _____

4. What do people probably use half-and-half for? How do you know? _____

    _____

5. How big is one serving of mayonnaise? _____

6. How many servings are in a can of green beans? _____

7. How much raw rice do you need for one serving of cooked rice? _____

    _____

8. How many calories are in a serving of rice? _____

9. Which of these four foods contain the most calories per serving? _____

10. What percentage (%) of the RDA (recommended daily allowance) of protein is in
    one-half cup of rice? _____

11. How many grams of protein are in one serving of rice? _____

12. How many different vitamins and minerals does the rice contain? _____

13. What chemical additives do you see on these labels? _____

    _____

14. Your doctor says that too much cholesterol is bad for your health. Can you eat
    this mayonnaise? Why or why not? _____

    _____

Going Beyond the Text

Bring some food labels to class. Work in pairs. Ask and answer questions about the
labels. (Use questions like those above.) Which food is the most fattening? Which is the
most healthful? Which has the most artificial additives? Tell the class.

PART FIVE

PERSONAL STORIES

Follow these steps for the story:

1. Read it quickly and tell the main ideas.
2. Answer your instructor's questions about the story, or ask and answer questions of your own.
3. Tell your opinions of the ideas in the story.
4. Tell or write your own story about food or dieting.

My Diet

  I try to stay healthy, so I almost never eat junk food, and I don't usually go to fast-food places. I read a lot of articles in magazines about health, and I'm taking a nutrition course at the local college. But I have a problem. I worry too much about health. I know that poor nutrition causes sickness. When my professor gives a lecture about vitamin C, I worry that I need more of it in my diet. I begin to eat *lots* of oranges. Then she gives a lecture on cholesterol, and I worry that I have too much of it in my diet. I don't want to have a heart attack, so I eat *no* eggs, butter, or cream and almost no red meat. Then I read about the importance of fiber, and I worry again. Maybe I don't have enough of it in my diet. So I start to eat *lots* of cereal, whole wheat bread, and so on.

I can't relax when I worry about my health. Then I get depressed. Unfortunately, depression has a powerful effect on me. When I feel depressed, I also feel a strong need to eat junk food. I get some cola, a big bag of potato chips, a hot dog, and some chocolate chip cookies. I eat and eat and eat. Then, of course, I feel more depressed than before!

4

GETTING AROUND THE COMMUNITY

PART ONE

"HOW CAN I GET TO THE POST OFFICE?"

Getting Started

Look at the picture and talk about it.

1. Who are the two young travelers? What are they doing? What is their problem?
2. What are the other people in the picture doing?
3. Does this situation ever happen to you? Do you use a map or ask for directions—or both? Do people sometimes ask you for directions? What do you answer?

Preparing to Read

Think about the answers to these questions. (The reading selection will answer them.)

1. How do people in different places give directions?
2. Sometimes you ask, "How can I get to the post office?" but the person does not know the answer. What might he or she do?
3. How can body language help you?

Glancing at Vocabulary (optional)

Here are some vocabulary items from the reading selection. You can learn them now or come back to them later.

Nouns	Verbs	Adjectives	Expressions
map	find out	straight	to have a good time
travel	follow	flat	to have no idea
directions		polite	
customs		lost	
situations			

Read the following selection quickly. Then answer the questions after the reading.

"How Can I Get to the Post Office?"

A   I have a special rule for travel: never carry a map. I prefer to ask for directions. Sometimes I get lost, but I usually have a good time. I can practice a new language, meet new people, and learn new customs. And I find out about different "styles" of directions every time I ask, "How can I get to the post office?"

B   Foreign tourists are often confused in Japan because most streets there don't have names; in Japan, people use landmarks in their directions instead of street names. For example, the Japanese will say to travelers, "Go straight down to the corner. Turn left at the big hotel and go past a fruit market. The post office is across from the bus stop."

C   In the countryside of the American Midwest, there are not usually many landmarks. There are no mountains, so the land is very flat; in many places there are no towns or buildings within miles. Instead of landmarks, people will tell you directions and distances. In Kansas or Iowa, for instance, people will say, "Go north two miles. Turn east, and then go another mile."

D   People in Los Angeles, California, have no idea of distance on the map: they measure distance in Los Angeles in time, not miles. "How far away is the post office?" you ask. "Oh," they answer, "it's about five minutes from here." You say, "Yes, but how many miles away is it?" They don't know.

E   People in Greece sometimes do not even try to give directions because tourists seldom understand the Greek language. Instead, a Greek will often say, "Follow me." Then he'll lead you through the streets of the city to the post office.

F   Sometimes a person doesn't know the answer to your question. What happens in this situation? A New Yorker might say, "Sorry, I have no idea." But in Yucatan, Mexico, no one answers, "I don't know." People in Yucatan believe that "I don't know" is impolite. They usually give an answer, often a wrong one. A tourist can get very, very lost in Yucatan!

G   One thing will help you everywhere—in Japan, the United States, Greece, Mexico, or any other place. You might not understand a person's words, but you can probably understand the person's body language: He or she will usually turn and then point in the correct direction. Go in that direction, and you may find the post office!

Getting the Main Ideas

Write T (true) or F (false) on the lines.

1. _____   Travelers can learn about people's customs by asking questions about directions.

2. _____   People in different places always give directions in the same way: they use street names.

3. _____   People in some places give directions in miles, but people in other places give directions in time.

4. _____   In some places, people show travelers the way.

5. _____   People never give wrong directions.

6. _____   A person's body language can help you understand directions.

Guessing Meaning from Context

Sometimes examples of the meaning of a new vocabulary item are in another sentence or in another part of the sentence. The words *for example, for instance,* and *such as* are clues to meaning through examples.

Example: People in Los Angeles usually talk about *distance in time.* They'll say things such as, "The post office is about five minutes from here." (An example of *distance in time* is "five minutes from here.")

A. Write examples for the underlined words in the following sentences on the lines.

1. In Japan, people use <u>landmarks</u> in their directions. For example, the Japanese will say, "Go straight down to the corner. Turn left at the big hotel and go past the fruit market. The post office is across from the bus stop."

_____

2.   People will tell you <u>directions</u> and <u>distances</u>. In Kansas or Iowa, for instance, they will say, "Go north two miles. Turn east, and then go another mile."

directions: _____

distances: _____

3.   You can probably understand a person's <u>body language</u>. He or she will usually turn and then point in the correct direction.

_____

Sometimes details about a vocabulary item give clues to its meaning.

B.   Find the answers to the questions about the underlined word in the following sentences. Write them on the lines.

In the <u>countryside</u> of the American Midwest, there are not usually many landmarks. The land is very flat, and there are no towns or buildings within miles.

1.   What kind of thing is "the countryside"? _____

2.   How does it look? _____

3.   What doesn't it have? _____

4.   What does the word *countryside* mean? _____

_____

Recognizing Reading Structure

A.   In the reading selection, there is a capital letter next to each of the seven paragraphs. In this exercise, write the main topic of each paragraph next to its letter. (A and B have answers.)

A: Introduction   E: _____

B: Directions in Japan   F: _____

C: _____   G: _____

D: _____

B.   Circle the number of the *one* main idea of the reading.

1.   There are not many landmarks in the American Midwest.
2.   Never carry a map for travel.
3.   There are different ways to give directions in different parts of the world.
4.   New Yorkers often say, "I have no idea," but people in Yucatan, Mexico, never say this.

Understanding Details

Punctuation often provides clues to the meaning of sentences and paragraphs. A colon (:) or a semicolon (;) can separate two closely related sentences. The second sentence usually explains or adds information to the meaning of the first sentence.

Example: In Japan, most streets don't have names; people use landmarks in their directions. (Streets don't have names. For this reason, people use landmarks.)

Commas (,) can separate items in a series.

Example: In Japan, people use landmarks in their directions: They talk about hotels, markets, and bus stops. (What are some examples of landmarks? Hotels, markets, and bus stops.)

Quotation marks separate direct quotes (people's exact words) from the rest of the sentence.

Example: Instead, a Greek will say, "Follow me." (What words does a Greek often use instead of directions? "Follow me.")

Find the answers to these questions in the reading selection. Write them on the lines.

1. The writer of the reading selection has a special rule for travel. What is it?

   _____

2. Why are foreign tourists often confused in Japan?

   _____

3. What are some examples of Japanese directions?

   _____

   _____

4. What directions will people give travelers in the American Midwest? (Give examples.)

   _____

   _____

5. Why don't people in Los Angeles give directions in miles?

   _____

6. How do Greeks give directions? Why?

   _____

7. People in Yucatan, Mexico, give directions differently from people in New York. Explain this statement.

    _____

    _____

8. How does a person give directions with body language?

    _____

    _____

Now turn back to the "Preparing to Read" section on page 45 and answer the questions.

Discussing the Reading

Talk about your answers to the following questions.

1. Do you travel a lot? How do you ask for directions?
2. How do people give directions in your country (by landmarks, in miles, or ...)?
3. Where do you live now? How do people give directions here?
4. How can you use body language in directions?
5. In your opinion, why do people in different places give directions in different ways?

PART TWO

LAWS

Glancing at Vocabulary (optional)

Here are some vocabulary items from the next reading selection. You can learn them now or come back to them later.

Nouns	Verbs	Adjectives	Expressions
ticket	murder	similar	against the law
fine	steal	illegal	police officer
law	cross	legal	in public
liquor		local	
alcohol		strange	
crosswalk			

Skimming for Main Ideas

Read the following paragraphs quickly. Remember to read in phrases (several words at a time). Then circle the number of the main idea of each paragraph.

Laws

A   Most laws in the United States and Canada are similar to laws in other countries. For example, it is against the law everywhere to murder a person, and it is illegal to steal money. Everyone knows these laws, but immigrants, foreign students, or tourists in a new country may not know some of the local laws. Different places may have different laws: A legal act in Brazil, Korea, or France might be illegal in Toronto, Miami, or San Francisco.

1. It is against the law to murder a person or to steal.
2. Visitors do not always know the local laws of a new place.
3. Laws are usually different in different countries.

B   In many cities in the United States, for instance, it is not legal to "jaywalk." This law may seem strange to visitors. Sometimes they cross a street, and a police officer gives them a ticket. Then they need to pay a fine of $10 to $25 within ten days. They soon learn to cross a street only in a crosswalk or at a corner. It's against the law to cross in the middle of the street.

1. It's illegal to jaywalk in many American cities.
2. Foreign visitors get a lot of tickets.
3. Foreign students think local laws are strange.

C   Most people know that states in the United States have different laws about the legal drinking age; this age varies, but in most states no one under twenty-one can buy alcohol, even beer or wine. Also, in most U.S. cities, it is illegal to drink alcohol in public. Of course, liquor is legal in restaurants and bars, but it's against the law to drink a can of beer, for instance, on a public street. Some people put the can in a paper bag and drink; nobody can see the beer, but it still isn't legal. In addition, it is illegal to have an open liquor bottle inside a car.

1. In most American cities, you may drink liquor only in homes, restaurants, and bars.
2. It is against the law for people under twenty-one to drink wine.
3. States and cities in the United States have different laws about alcohol.

Now read the selections again. Try to guess the meanings of new words from the context. Use your dictionary only when absolutely necessary.

Discussing the Reading

Talk about your answers to the following questions.

1. Is it illegal in your country to "jaywalk" or to drink on public streets?
2. Does your city, state, province, or country have a legal drinking age? What is it?
3. In your opinion, why do many cities have these laws?
4. How are some U.S. or Canadian laws different from laws in your country? What U.S. or Canadian laws surprise you?

PART THREE

BUILDING VOCABULARY; STUDY SKILLS

> You can often guess the meaning of a word from its context. It helps to know the "part of speech": Is it a noun, a verb, an adjective, an adverb, or a preposition? Sometimes you can tell the part of speech from the *suffix* (the ending) on the word. Some common suffixes are:
>
> -able
> -al
> -ical
> -ic   } usually indicate adjectives
> -ar
> -ful
>
> -er
> -or
> -ist
> -sion   } usually indicate nouns
> -tion
> -ment
> -ness

A. Are the following words nouns or adjectives? The suffixes will tell you. On the lines, write _n_ (noun) or _adj_ (adjective).

1. ____	practical	7. ____	recreation	13. ____	ethnic
2. ____	formal	8. ____	national	14. ____	healthful
3. ____	management	9. ____	legal	15. ____	direction
4. ____	tourist	10. ____	enrollment	16. ____	physical
5. ____	spectacular	11. ____	available	17. ____	discussion
6. ____	academic	12. ____	professor	18. ____	astrological

B. In each of the following sections, fill in the blank with the correct form—noun, verb, or adjective. Choose from the words above each section.

competition	competitor	compete	competitive

1. Vegetarians are not usually _____ people.
2. Students often have to _____ for grades.
3. McDonald's and Burger King are _____s in the fast-food business; they are in _____ with each other.

management	manager	manage	manageable

4. Her major at the university is business _____ .
5. Who is going to _____ the new health-food store?
6. A man from the Midwest is going to be the new _____ .
7. I'm afraid this is not a _____ problem.

forgetfulness	forget	forgetful

8. Why do I always _____ new vocabulary items?
9. I am a very _____ person.
10. _____ is a big problem for me.

Study Skill: Using a Dictionary (Parts of Speech)

If possible, everyone in the class should use the same kind of dictionary for these exercises. Work quickly. The first student with the correct answers is the winner. Find the following words in your dictionary. Write _n_ on the lines before the nouns, _v_ before the verbs, _adj_ before the adjectives, and _adv_ before the adverbs. Some words function as more than one part of speech and so have different meanings.

1. ___ different	11. ___ special	21. ___ confused
2. ___ seldom	12. ___ usually	22. ___ new
3. ___ foreign	13. ___ legally	23. ___ daily
4. ___ grass	14. ___ fish	24. ___ park
5. ___ stop	15. ___ right	25. ___ construction
6. ___ work	16. ___ turn	26. ___ danger
7. ___ adult	17. ___ load	27. ___ sale
8. ___ beware	18. ___ pedestrian	28. ___ wet
9. ___ trespass	19. ___ crossing	29. ___ detour
10. ___ telephone	20. ___ discount	30. ___ paint

PART FOUR

SCANNING FOR INFORMATION

Look at the picture. Match the words to the signs. Put the correct numbers on the signs.

1. Telephone
2. Wet Paint
3. Stop
4. Put Litter Here
5. Ped Xing
6. People Working
7. Keep Off the Grass
8. Beware of Dog
9. Sale! Big Discounts!
10. Restrooms
11. Loading Zone
12. No Fishing
13. Adult Only
14. No Trespassing

Going Beyond the Text

For several days, read all the signs on your way home or to school. Write down the words. Then write the words from some of the signs on the blackboard. Discuss their meanings with the class.

PERSONAL STORIES

Follow these steps for the story:

1. Read it quickly and tell the main idea.
2. Answer your instructor's questions about the story, or ask and answer questions of your own.
3. Tell your own opinions of the ideas in the story.
4. Tell or write about your own neighborhood.

My American Neighborhood

I live in an apartment building. There are a lot of immigrants in the building. My next-door neighbor is a Russian lady with two cats. In the apartment above mine there is a family from the Philippines. In the summer they sometimes barbecue meat outside on their balcony; it smells wonderful. A Mexican couple lives down the hall from me. They have three kids who seem very American. For example, their parents always speak to them in Spanish, but they answer in English.

There's a fast-food place across the street from my building, but the food is terrible. Fortunately, there's an Indian restaurant just two blocks down the street; the food is very spicy, but I like it a lot. Another restaurant around the corner from my place has a strange sign: Italian/Chinese/American Food. What country do the owners come from? I have no idea!

There is a liquor store on the corner. The owner is a nice man from Iran. Unfortunately, almost once a month someone tries to steal money from him. He can't ever relax. Why doesn't he find a different job?

The local adult school is straight down the street about five blocks. The campus of the school isn't beautiful, but it's my favorite place in the neighborhood. It has a friendly atmosphere. The school offers classes in English, typing, history, computers, auto mechanics, and so on. Some of the students are Americans, but most are nonnative speakers of English. Many are refugees or immigrants, and a few are here on a student visa. We all have a lot in common. We're trying to learn a strange new language. Sometimes we're depressed and homesick, but we usually have a good time in class.

I have one big problem. I want to practice English, but most people in my "American" neighborhood don't speak it!

5

HOUSING AND
THE FAMILY

WOMEN IN THE NUCLEAR FAMILY

Getting Started

Look at the pictures and talk about them.

1. Where and when does (did) each scene take place? What are the people doing?
2. How are these scenes similar to ones in your country? How are they different?
3. Is your family similar to any family on these pages?
4. How do you think family life is changing these days?

Preparing to Read

Think about the answers to these questions. (The reading selection will answer them.)

1. How is family structure changing throughout the world?
2. What are the advantages of a nuclear family?
3. What are the disadvantages?
4. According to studies, why are women generally less satisfied with marriage than men are?

Glancing at Vocabulary (optional)

Here are some vocabulary items from the reading selection. You can learn them now or come back to them later.

Nouns	Verbs	Adverbs
group	change	generally
structure	share	actually
advantage		
freedom	**Adjectives**	**Expressions**
relative	main	nuclear family
power	married	head of the family
housework	well-educated	make decisions
child care	satisfied	full-time job
disadvantage		
marriage		

Read the following selection quickly. Then answer the questions after the reading.

Women in the Nuclear Family

A   The family is changing. In the past, grandparents, parents, and children used to live together; in other words, they had an "extended family." Sometimes two or more brothers with their wives and children were part of this large family group. But family structure is changing throughout the world. The "nuclear family" consists of only one father, one mother, and children; it is becoming the main family structure everywhere.

B   The nuclear family offers married women some advantages: They have freedom from their relatives, and the husband does not have all the power of the family. Family structure in most parts of the world is still "patriarchal"; that is, the father is the head of the family and makes most of the important decisions. Studies show, however, that in nuclear families, men and women usually make an equal number of decisions about family life. Also, well-educated husbands and wives often prefer to share the power.

C   But wives usually have to "pay" for the benefits of freedom and power. When women lived in extended families, sisters, grandmothers, and aunts helped one another with housework and child care. In addition, older women in a large family group had important positions. Wives in nuclear families do not enjoy this benefit, and they have another disadvantage, too: Women generally live longer than their husbands, so older women from nuclear families often have to live alone.

D   Studies show that women are generally less satisfied with marriage than men are. In the past, men worked outside the home and women worked inside. Housework and child care were a full-time job, and there was no time for anything else. Of course, this situation is changing. Women now work outside the home and seem to have more freedom than they did in the past. Why, then, are some women still discontent?

E   In most parts of the world today, women work because the family needs more money. However, their outside jobs often give them less freedom, not more, because they still have to do most of the housework. The women actually have two full-time jobs—one outside the home and another inside—and not much free time.

F   The nuclear family will probably continue to be the main family form of the future. Change, however, usually brings disadvantages along with benefits, and the family forms of the past had many advantages.

Getting the Main Ideas

Write T (true) or F (false) on the lines.

1. _____   Families around the world are generally smaller than they used to be.

2. _____   In most countries, wives have most of the power in the family.

3. _____   Living in a nuclear family is both good and bad for a woman.

4. _____   Women in extended families used to help each other with the housework and the children.

5. _____   Generally, women are happy with marriage, but men are not satisfied.

6. _____   Women with jobs are the most satisfied because they have freedom from housework.

Guessing Meaning from Context

Sometimes a word (or words) in another sentence or in another part of the sentence has the opposite meaning of a new vocabulary item.

Example: Studies show that women are generally not as happy about marriage as men. Why are they *dissatisfied?* (*Dissatisfied* has a similar meaning to "not happy"; in other words, it is the opposite of "happy." *Dissatisfied* means "unhappy.")

A. On the lines, write the words or expressions with opposite meanings to the underlined words.

1. In the past, grandparents, parents, and children used to live together in one <u>extended family</u>. But family structure is changing throughout the world. The nuclear family is becoming the main family structure everywhere.

   _____

2. Wives in nuclear families do not often enjoy this <u>benefit</u>, and they have another disadvantage, too.

   _____

3. Generally, studies show that women are less satisfied with marriage than men are. Why are they <u>discontent</u>?

   _____

Sometimes an explanation or an equivalent (equal) of a new vocabulary item is in another part of the sentence. The phrases *in other words* and *that is* are clues to an explanation.

Example: Many women work both outside the home and inside; in other words, they have two *full-time jobs*. (What are their two jobs? Work outside the home and work at home.)

B. On the lines, complete the explanations of the underlined words in the following sentences.

1. In the past, grandparents, parents, and children used to live together; in other words, they had an <u>extended family</u>.

   An extended family is a living group of _____

   _____

2. Family structure in most parts of the world is still <u>patriarchal</u>; that is, the father is the head of the family and makes most of the important decisions.

   In a patriarchal family, _____

   _____

Recognizing Reading Structure

A. In the reading selection, there is a capital letter next to each of the six paragraphs. In this exercise, match each paragraph with its topic. Write the correct letter on the line.

1. _____ The changing family structure

2. _____ Comparison of women's work in the past and in the present

3. _____   Why many women are dissatisfied with their work

4. _____   The advantages of the nuclear family for women

5. _____   The disadvantages of the nuclear family

6. _____   Conclusion or summary

B. Circle the number of the *one* main idea of the reading.

1. The nuclear family structure offers women both advantages and disadvantages.
2. Women are generally less satisfied with marriage than men are.
3. Family structure in most parts of the world is still patriarchal.
4. Family structure is changing throughout the world.

Understanding Details

Transition words (*in other words, that is, also, in addition, however,* and so on) often provide clues to the meaning of sentences and paragraphs.

Examples: In the past, grandparents, parents, and children used to live together. *In addition,* sometimes brothers with their families were part of this extended family. (In other words, grandparents, parents, children, brothers, and the brothers' families all lived together.)

Women have more freedom in the nuclear family. This freedom, *however,* can be a disadvantage. (Because freedom is usually an advantage, the idea of a "disadvantage" is not expected. The second sentence presents a contrast to the first.)

Punctuation often provides clues to the meaning of sentences and paragraphs. Italics (a slanted kind of print) sometimes emphasize words.

Example: Most women work because the family needs *money,* not because they need more freedom. (*Money* is the important word in the sentence because it is in contrast to *freedom.*)

Quotation marks can introduce a new word or indicate a special use of a word or expression.

Example: Wives usually have to "pay" for the benefits of freedom and power. (The word *pay* usually refers to money. It has a different meaning in this sentence.)

Circle the letter of the correct answer to each of the following questions, according to the reading selection.

1.   Who used to live together in an "extended family"?

   a.   There were only grandparents and children.
   b.   There was one father, one mother, and their children.
   c.   There were many relatives.

2.   What advantages does the nuclear family offer women?

   a.   The women have more freedom and can share in decisions.
   b.   The women do not have to be the heads of the family.
   c.   The women's relatives do not help them with the housework and child care.

3.   What are some disadvantages of the nuclear family for women?

   a.   Husbands have to share power with their wives and help them with the housework.
   b.   Older women do not often have important positions and often live alone when their husbands die.
   c.   Family structure is more patriarchal in the nuclear family.

4.   Why are many women dissatisfied with marriage and the nuclear family?

   a.   They want to stay home and do the housework.
   b.   They do not have enough money.
   c.   They have too much work and not much free time.

Now turn back to the "Preparing to Read" section on page 59 and answer the questions.

Discussing the Reading

Talk about your answers to the following questions.

1.   Do you live in a nuclear family or in an extended family? What is the main family structure in your country?
2.   What do you think is good about nuclear families? What is good about extended families?
3.   Who is the head of your family? In your opinion, is it good or bad for husbands and wives to share power in the family?
4.   In your opinion, is it good for a married woman to work outside the home? Why or why not?
5.   Who does most of the housework in your home? In your opinion, is it good or bad for husbands and wives to share housework?

PART TWO

EVENINGS WITH THE FAMILY: PRESENT AND PAST

Glancing at Vocabulary (optional)

Here are some vocabulary items from the next reading selection. You can learn them now or come back to them later.

Nouns	Verbs	Adjectives	Expressions
screen	argue	quiet	"boob tube"
porch	disappear	pleasant	center of attention
breeze	stare		spend evenings
fan	rock		air conditioning
pause	clean		back and forth
lesson	reappear		social center
fan			small talk

Skimming for Main Ideas

Read the following three paragraphs quickly. Remember to read in phrases. Then circle the number of the main idea of each paragraph.

Evenings with the Family: Present and Past

A   What happens to the typical American family every evening after dinner? First, everyone argues about the dishes. Then they disappear into the living room. They sit there for the rest of the evening. They are quiet; nobody says anything to anyone. They stare at a small screen until their eyes are tired and red. The "boob tube" is the center of attention.

1.   Americans argue about dishes.
2.   Television influences family life in the United States.
3.   Television causes red eyes.

B   When I was a child, we used to spend hot summer evenings on the front porch. We didn't have air conditioning, and the house was always too warm, but there was usually a cool, pleasant breeze out on the porch. We children used to play games or read comic books there while my father sat in his rocking chair and rocked back and forth for hours. Sometimes he smoked his pipe or did the crossword puzzle from the newspaper. Mother used a paper fan when there was no breeze. Sometimes she cleaned strawberries. Then later in the evening, she used to take them into the kitchen and reappear in a few minutes with big dishes of strawberries and cream.

1. The front porch used to be a nice place for the family in the summer.
2. The front porch was always very hot in the summer.
3. My parents usually read the newspaper on the porch in the summer.

C   The front porch was also a kind of social center. There were special "rules" for evenings on the porch. Everyone knew the rules, but nobody said anything about them. For example, when people in our town took walks on summer evenings, they often used to stop for a moment at the bottom step of our porch. This pause was almost a social rule; it was like a knock on the front door. Then my father always said, "Come on up and sit down!" This was another "rule": He always used those exact words. Then Mother brought out lemonade or iced tea—never coffee or juice or alcohol. Everyone talked about the local baseball team, gardening, and the hot weather; we children learned our first lessons in small talk on the porch.

1. People talked only about important things on our porch.
2. There were certain social "rules" on the front porch.
3. We never used to drink coffee or alcohol.

Carefully read the selection again. Try to guess the meanings of the new words from the context. Use your dictionary only when absolutely necessary.

Viewpoint

In many reading selections, authors give a point of view; that is, they give their opinions about the topic. Sometimes they write their viewpoints clearly, but more often they only imply (suggest) opinions.

What is the viewpoint of the author of the reading selection "Evenings with the Family: Present and Past"? Circle one of the words in parentheses.

1. I believe that the author (likes / dislikes) evenings at home in front of the TV set.
2. She (liked / disliked) summer evenings on the front porch when she was a child.

Why did you circle those words? Give reasons from the reading.

Discussing the Reading

Talk about your answers to the following questions.

1.   What does your family do in the evenings after dinner? Is this typical in your country? Was it typical twenty years ago?
2.   Do you watch much television? What do you think about it?
3.   Is there a special "social center" in your house? Where is it? What do you do there?

PART THREE

BUILDING VOCABULARY; STUDY SKILLS

A.   In each column, which word does not belong? Cross it out. Explain your decisions.

1. kitchen	2. coffee	3. breeze	4. housework
screen	lemonade	hot	child care
porch	iced tea	cool	gardening
living room	strawberries	warm	social

B.   Match each word on the left with its meaning on the right. Write the correct letter on the line.

1. _____	quiet	a. to come back
2. _____	"boob tube"	b. conversation about unimportant things
		c. not talking; with no sound
3. _____	stare	d. something to make a breeze
4. _____	rock	e. television
		f. to wait or stop
5. _____	breeze	g. to move back and forth
6. _____	fan	h. to look at
		i. a small wind
7. _____	reappear	j. to fight; not to agree
8. _____	pause	
9. _____	argue	
10. _____	small talk	

Sometimes you can tell what part of speech a vocabulary item is by the suffix on the end of a word. Some common suffixes are:

Nouns	Adjective	Adverb
-ance	-y	-ly
-ence	-ive	

C. In each of the following sections, fill in the blanks with the correct form—noun, verb, adjective, or adverb. Choose from the words above each section.

argument	argue	argumentative

1. We had a terrible _____ last night about the dishes.
2. My sister always _____s with me about TV.
3. I think she is an _____ person.

typical	typically

4. _____ , my father did crossword puzzles in the evening.
5. A _____ American family watches a lot of TV.

breeze	breezy

6. There was usually a cool _____ on the porch.
7. I liked to sit outside on a _____ evening.

disappear	disappearance

8. When my mother brought out strawberries and cream, they used to

   _____ very quickly.

9. She was always happy about their _____ .

Study Skill: Increasing Reading Speed (Reading in Phrases)

> Reading speed is important to students. Fast readers usually understand reading material better than slow readers. They usually read several words (a phrase) at a time. You can improve your reading speed with practice.

In the following reading, which words belong together? Read the sentences in phrases. (There may be several correct possibilities.) Separate the phrases with lines.

When you want|to rent|a house or apartment,|you need to look at the classified ads in the newspaper. These ads are in sections such as "Apartments—Unfurnished," "Apartments—Furnished," "Houses," and so on. In large city newspapers, the ads for each area of the city appear together. Each ad gives information about the apartment or house: for instance, the amount of rent, the location, the size of the place, the cost of utilities (electricity, gas, heat), and the furnishings. Because the ad is usually small, this information is in the form of abbreviations (short forms of words).

PART FOUR

SCANNING FOR INFORMATION

Look at the following classified ads. They are all for rented apartments and houses. Read the questions about the ads and find the information as fast as you can.

Here are common abbreviations in rental ads:

air = air conditioning
bd (or bedr) = bedroom
blk = block
bltins = built-ins (The refrigerator and stove are already there.)
frplc = fireplace
furn = furnished (The apartment has furniture.)
gt = great
htd = heated
loc = location
m/f = male or female
nu cpts/drps = new carpets and drapes
rec = recreation

sec bldg = secured building (has locks or a guard at the main entrance)
sgl (or bach) = single (or bachelor) apartment; there is no bedroom; instead, the sofa in the living room becomes a bed
stv/ref (or stv/frig) = stove/ refrigerator
unf = unfurnished (The apartment does not have furniture.)
util = utilities (gas, electricity, water)
w = with
yd = yard

Check all the *true* statements about the ads.

1. Building 1 offers an apartment with
   a. _____   furniture
   b. _____   carpets and drapes
   c. _____   a stove and refrigerator
   d. _____   one bedroom
   e. _____   rent of $290 per month

2. Building 2
   a. _____   has some single apartments
   b. _____   has some one- or two-bedroom apartments
   c. _____   has furnished apartments
   d. _____   has new carpets and drapes
   e. _____   has a stove and refrigerator
   f. _____   is a good place for a child

3. Building 3
   a. _____   has one-bedroom apartments for $355 per month
   b. _____   is near shopping areas
   c. _____   is a safe (security) building
   d. _____   is good for a person without a car

4. Building 4
   a. _____   has two-bedroom apartments for $590 per month
   b. _____   seems to have many apartments
   c. _____   has apartments with fireplaces
   d. _____   allows dogs and cats
   e. _____   has a heated pool
   f. _____   has a gymnasium

1.

> **APT. UNF.-CITY—S.W.   7450**
> $290-Sgl, utils.paid. Carpets, drapes,stv/frig. 213/641-6831

2.

> **APT. UNF.-CITY WEST   7550**
> GRT.LOC.1&2Bd.,nu crpts/drp, air, bltins, rec.area,childs play yd.533 S.Harvard213/383-1122

3.

> **APT. FUR.-CITY-WEST   6550**
> A TOUCH OF CHARM
> You'll love ...Newly decorated & furn.$355-385 w/bright full kitchens. Ibrm $475. Security quiet bldg.Low move-in. Buses shopping 1 blk. Wilshire 5 blks 155 S Manhattan,213/462-5720

4.

> Hollywd & Hollywd Hills
> **KINGS ROAD APARTMENTS**
> A Happy Place To Live
> Bachelors m/f Furn From $400
> Singles From $450
> 1 Bdrms Furn/Unf. From $590
> 2 Bedrooms From $800
> 2 Bedrooms & Loft From $900
> FURN & UNFURN.
> —Fireplace
> —Htd pool, health spa & gym
> —No pets
> Eq. Hsng.
> HOURS 9-6 DAILY
> 733 N. KINGS RD.
> (213) 653-3337
> Managed By Ring Bros.

Going Beyond the Text

Bring several classified ads for houses and apartments to class. List the abbreviations and then find out their meanings.

Read some of the ads aloud. Is anyone in the class looking for housing? Help that person choose an ad.

PART FIVE

PERSONAL STORIES

Follow these steps for the story:

1. Read it quickly and tell the main idea.
2. Answer your instructor's questions about the story, or ask and answer questions of your own.
3. Tell your own opinions of the ideas in the story.
4. Tell or write about your own house or apartment.

Our New House

My family and I lived in an apartment until last spring. We weren't happy there. The building was crowded and noisy, and the manager didn't use to fix things. We decided to move. But most available apartments in this city were even worse, and the rent was higher. So we started to look for a house to buy.

It was very difficult to find a house! Homes in quiet, pleasant neighborhoods were too expensive. We found a few inexpensive houses, but the areas were dangerous. Prices in all areas seemed to go up every day, and we needed to find a place fast. We began to get nervous.

Finally, my husband and I found a small house in a neighborhood that wasn't bad. The problem was the house itself. It was ugly. It needed paint. The wallpaper was horrible; there were scenes of hunting and fishing all over the bedroom walls! The carpet was in terrible condition, and it was *orange*. The porch and roof needed repairs. The "garden" consisted of dirt, weeds, and a few half-dead plants with insects all over them. When our kids first saw their new home, they burst into tears. I understood that. I wanted to cry too.

Well, the four of us made a decision to share the work and spend our summer vacation on the house. We cleaned up the yard and painted the house. We fixed the porch and roof. We removed the ugly wallpaper and carpet. We planted trees and grass. Day by day, this horrible little house became our *home*. We're happy here. The kids are content— except for one thing. Now it's their job to cut the grass every weekend.

6

EMERGENCIES AND STRANGE EXPERIENCES

PART ONE

A MURDER MYSTERY: THE CRITIC IN THE STORM

Getting Started

Look at the picture and talk about it.

1. What kind of story is this scene from?
2. What happened to the man on the floor? How does he look?
3. Who is the man by the door? How does he feel?
4. Who is the other man? What is he doing? How does he feel?

72

Preparing to Read

Think about the answers to the following questions. (The reading selection will answer them.)

1. Who was Edward Grimsley? What was he doing at the beginning of the story?
2. Who came to see him late one night? Why? What was the problem?
3. Who was Ambrose Pennwright? How did he die?
4. What did Grimsley see in Pennwright's room?

Glancing at Vocabulary (optional)

Here are some vocabulary items from the reading selection. You can learn them now or come back to them later.

Nouns	Adjectives	Expressions
detective	well-known	face down
vacation	heavy	butter knife
guest	surprised	out of place
article	loud	
police	unfortunate	
	alive	
Verbs		
hit	**Adverb**	
chase	nervously	
shake		
bite		
die		
lie		

Read the following selection quickly. Then answer the questions after the reading.

A Murder Mystery: The Critic in the Storm

A Edward Grimsley, the world-famous detective, was spending his vacation on a small Caribbean island. There were beautiful beaches and facilities for water sports and other recreation near his hotel. In addition, at Grimsley's hotel there was a meeting of people in the restaurant business. Thus, because Grimsley enjoyed good food almost as much as he enjoyed a good mystery, the island was the perfect place for Grimsley's vacation. The only disadvantage was the time of year: the hurricane season.

B On Grimsley's second night at the hotel, a powerful storm hit the sleepy little island. Strong winds and heavy rains chased the tourists inside, and as a result most people were sitting nervously in their rooms. Therefore, Grimsley was surprised by the knock on his door at 11:00 P.M., at the height of the hurricane.

C The hotel manager was standing there. He looked worried. His hands were shaking, and he was biting his lip. The wind outside was very loud; thus, when he spoke, he had to shout.

D   "Mr. Grimsley," he said, "we have a problem here at the hotel. I know this is your vacation, but you are a detective, and I hope you can help us. A hotel guest died this evening: Mr. Ambrose Pennwright."

E   "The famous food critic?" asked Grimsley. "Well, well. Mr. Pennwright is—er, *was*—quite well-known for his newspaper articles about restaurants. This is very interesting. How did he die?"

F   The manager shrugged his shoulders and looked a little lost. "Of course," he said, "it's possible that he had a heart attack. But I'm afraid that possibly someone murdered him. The telephone lines are down from the storm, so we can't call the police yet. Can you help us?"

G   Grimsley followed the manager to the room of the unfortunate restaurant critic. Ambrose Pennwright's very large body was lying face down on the floor next to a small table. A bottle of wine, a glass, a plate with cheese, some caviar, and a butter knife were on the table, but there did not seem to be a gun, a sharp knife, or any other weapon anywhere. Nothing in the room seemed out of place, but Grimsley felt there was something strange about the atmosphere. He examined the body for a minute, and he saw that Pennwright was not bleeding. There was a very small piece of caviar on the critic's lower lip.

H   "Who found the body?" Grimsley asked the manager. "And who last saw him alive?"

I   "Please come with me," the manager said. "There are several people in my office. You ought to discuss the situation with them."

to be continued . . .

Getting the Main Ideas

Put the following events from the reading selection in the correct order. Which happened first? second? third? Write numbers from 1 through 6 on the lines.

_____   A hurricane hit the island.

_____   The manager told Grimsley about the death of Ambrose Pennwright, a restaurant critic.

_____   The manager wanted Grimsley to talk with some other people in his office.

_____   Edward Grimsley, a famous detective, went to a Caribbean island for a vacation.

_____   The hotel manager came to see Grimsley during the storm.

_____   Grimsley examined the room and the dead body.

Guessing Meaning from Context

Sometimes words in other sentences or in another part of the sentence are clues to the meaning of a new vocabulary item.

Example: Edward Grimsley was spending his vacation on a small Caribbean *island*. (Here are the clues to the meaning of the word *island:* It is small, it is in the Caribbean Sea, and people can spend their vacations on it. Therefore, an island is a place—a small piece of land in the middle of water.)

A. The questions after each of the following sentences will lead you to clues to the meaning of the underlined words. Find the answers and write them on the lines. Then circle the letter of the words that give the correct meaning of the underlined vocabulary items.

1. Edward Grimsley was spending his vacation on a small Caribbean island. There were beautiful <u>beaches</u> with facilities for water sports near his hotel.

    Where was Grimsley spending his vacation? _____

    What is an island? _____

    What activities are common near beaches? _____

    What are beaches?

    a. mountains for vacations   b. places near the sea   c. hotels for detectives

2. There was a small piece of <u>caviar</u> on the critic's lower <u>lip</u>. The nervous hotel manager was biting his lip.

    What body part has an upper and a lower section? _____

    What does a person bite when he or she is nervous? _____

    What is a lip?

    a. part of the mouth   b. part of the leg   c. a kind of food

    Where was the piece of caviar? _____

    What is caviar?

    a. a kind of clothing   b. blood   c. a kind of food

3. "How did he die?" asked Grimsley. The manager <u>shrugged his shoulders</u> and looked a little lost.

    What are shoulders? _____

    When did the manager shrug his shoulders? _____

    _____

Did he know the answer to Grimsley's question? How do you know? _____

_____

What does *shrug one's shoulders* mean?

   a. It is a movement of the body. It means "I don't know."
   b. It is an answer to a question. It means "I'll tell you later."
   c. It is an action. It answers a question about directions.

B. Which words in each of the following sentences give clues to the meanings of the underlined words? Circle the words. Then circle the letter of the word or words that give the correct meaning of the underlined vocabulary item.

   1. The wind outside was very (loud;) thus when he (spoke,) he had to shout.

       a. speak loudly   b. sing   c. explain the situation

   2. He looked worried. His hands were shaking, and he was biting his lip.

       a. relaxed   b. nervous   c. hungry

   3. "The world-famous food critic?" asked Grimsley. "He was quite well-known for his newspaper articles about restaurants."

       world-famous:

       a. traveling around the world
       b. known everywhere
       c. knowing everything about restaurants

       food critic:

       a. a person who does not like food
       b. a person who reads the newspaper
       c. a person who writes about restaurants

   4. There did not seem to be a gun, a sharp knife, or any other weapon anywhere.

       a. a kind of knife or gun
       b. a mystery
       c. something used to hurt or kill

   5. He examined the body for a minute, and he saw that Pennwright was not bleeding.

       a. looked at   b. listened to   c. talked to

       "Who found the body, and who last saw him alive?

       a. a weapon   b. a dead person   c. a living person

Understanding Details

Transitional words often provide clues to the meaning of sentences and paragraphs. The following words and expressions have similar meanings: Like the connecting word *so,* they all show an effect.

therefore	consequently	because of this
thus	as a result	for this reason

Example: There were beautiful beaches and facilities for water sports; *thus,* it was a perfect place for a vacation. (Because there were beautiful beaches and facilities for water sports, it was a perfect place for a vacation.)

A. Find the answer to each of the following questions from the reading selection. Write the answers on the lines.

1. Why were the tourists sitting nervously in their rooms?

   _____

2. Why was Grimsley surprised by the knock at the door of his hotel room?

   _____

3. Why was the hotel manager shouting at Grimsley?

   _____

4. Why didn't the hotel manager call the police?

   _____

B. Complete the following sentences. Circle the letters of *all* the correct phrases for each blank.

1. Edward Grimsley _____

   a. was a detective
   b. enjoyed good food
   c. enjoyed mysteries

   d. was in the restaurant business
   e. was on vacation

2. The advantages to the Caribbean island were _____

   a. the beaches
   b. the time of year
   c. the recreational facilities

   d. a hurricane
   e. the meeting of people in the restaurant business

3. Perhaps Ambrose Pennwright _____

   a. was still alive
   b. killed someone
   c. had a heart attack

   d. died because someone killed him
   e. died of a gunshot from the gun on the table in his room

4. Ambrose Pennwright was _____

   a. a detective
   b. dead
   c. famous as a food critic

   d. a small man
   e. bleeding

5. In Pennwright's room, Grimsley _____

   a. saw things out of place
   b. found the murder weapon
   c. felt something strange about the atmosphere

   d. called the police
   e. saw a piece of caviar on Pennwright's lip

Now turn back to the "Preparing to Read" section on page 73 and answer the questions.

Discussing the Reading

Talk about your answers to the following questions.

1. In your opinion, why was the hotel manager worried?
2. How many clues can you find in Pennwright's death? What are they?

PART TWO

A MURDER MYSTERY (continued)

Glancing at Vocabulary (optional)

Here are some vocabulary items from the next reading selection. You can learn them now or come back to them later.

Nouns	Verbs	Adjectives	Adverbs	Expressions
widow	cry	silent	terribly	gourmet food
owner	notice	calm	silently	restaurant
chef	introduce	poor	possibly	TV program
job	hate	natural		(show)
truth	taste	probable		
		terrible		
		honest		
		afraid		
		angry		

Skimming for Main Ideas

Read the following selection quickly. Then circle the number of the one main idea of each section.

A Murder Mystery (continued)

J   The manager led the detective to his office. Inside, there were two men and a woman. They were silent.

K   Althea Pennwright, Ambrose's widow, was not crying. In fact, she seemed quite calm and relaxed. She offered Edward Grimsley her hand.

L   "You're going to find my husband's murderer," she said. "How nice."

M   Next, Grimsley met Gregory Welles. Welles was the owner of a famous gourmet food restaurant in New York.

N   "Ambrose Pennwright was my best friend," Welles said, "and his murder is terribly unfortunate." Grimsley noticed a pleasant expression on Welles' face. There was no sign of sadness.

O   Then the manager introduced Grimsley to Horace Goodbody, a vegetarian chef with his own program called "How to Cook for Health."

P   "Ambrose was like a brother to me," Horace Goodbody said. "He got me the job on my TV show. I hope you find the killer soon." Goodbody's expression was similar to the widow's and the restaurant owner's; he didn't appear to be upset.

1. Althea Pennwright was Ambrose's widow.
2. Gregory Welles owned a gourmet restaurant in New York.
3. Horace Goodbody had a TV show about vegetarian cooking.
4. The three people in the hotel office did not seem upset about Ambrose's murder.

Q   Grimsley shook his head. "I'm confused," he said. "You're all talking about the *murder* of poor Mr. Pennwright, but nobody is sure it was murder. Possibly he died of natural causes."

R   Althea Pennwright stood up. Her face became hard and unpleasant. "A natural cause is possible, but I think murder is more probable. Do you want the truth? Everyone hated my husband. He was rich, intelligent, and powerful, but he was a terrible person. None of us is upset about his death. Unfortunately, we all have our reasons . . ."

S   Grimsley waited silently for a moment.

T   "Gregory Welles, for example, was afraid of my husband," Mrs. Pennwright continued. "The food in Mr. Welles' restaurant looks and tastes wonderful, but the quality is very poor. It contains chemicals and is worse than junk food. My husband found out and was writing an article about it when he came here.

U   Welles stared at her unhappily.

V   "Horace Goodbody," she continued, "is not an honest person. He has a very popular TV program. Every vegetarian in America watches it. However, in real life, Horace's diet consists mainly of fast food. His diet is not healthful. In fact, he isn't even a vegetarian. My husband was planning to tell the world about Mr. Goodbody in his next article. Horace knew this; thus, he was afraid to lose his TV show."

W   Goodbody had an unhappy expression on his face.

X   "And you, Mrs. Pennwright?" Mr. Grimsley asked. "Why did you hate your husband?"

1. The detective was confused about the three people in the office.
2. The three people all hated Ambrose Pennwright for different reasons.
3. Gregory Welles was afraid of Ambrose Pennwright because the food in Gregory's restaurant was not very good.
4. Horace Goodbody ate unhealthy fast food.

to be continued . . .

Discussing the Reading

Talk about your answers to the following questions.

1. Who were the suspects (the possible killers) in the murder of Ambrose Pennwright?
2. What were the suspects' motives (possible reasons for the murder)?
3. Who, in your opinion, was the murderer? Why do you think so?

PART THREE

BUILDING VOCABULARY; STUDY SKILLS

A. Circle the letters of *all* the words that might fit in each blank.

1. His expression was _____ .

   (a.) tired   (b.) calm   (c.) relaxed   d. silently

2. Her face _____ hard and unpleasant.

   a. hoped   b. looked   c. appeared   d. seemed

3. He stared _____ at her.

   a. silently   b. truth   c. angrily   d. unhappy

4. They have a _____ in New York.

   a. natural causes   b. TV show   c. restaurant   d. gourmet food

5. I hope that you _____ the killer soon.

   a. find   b. cry   c. die   d. offer

6. The manager introduced the detective to the _____ .

   a. widow   b. chef   c. owner   d. natural

7. _____ , we all hated him.

   a. Terribly   b. Unfortunately   c. In fact

8. The chef was afraid of my husband; _____ , he wanted to kill him.

   a. however   b. therefore   c. consequently   d. for this reason

B. Match the following words with their similar and opposite meanings. Write the correct letters on the lines.

SIMILAR MEANING

1. _____ famous   a. hurricane
2. _____ powerful   b. lost
                       c. strong
3. _____ cause   d. unfortunate
4. _____ murderer   e. well-known
                       f. killer
5. _____ storm   g. reason
6. _____ poor
7. _____ confused

OPPOSITE MEANING

1. _____ alive   a. terrible
2. _____ content   b. unhappy
                       c. calm
3. _____ loud   d. poor
4. _____ upset   e. stand up
                       f. dead
5. _____ wonderful   g. quiet
6. _____ rich
7. _____ lie down

The *prefix* (beginning) of a word often gives a clue to its meaning. Some prefixes give negative meanings to words; they create words with opposite meanings.

Examples: The *discontented* expression on his face told me that he was *unhappy.* (**Dis**contented is the opposite of *contented;* **un**happy is the opposite of *happy.*)

The following prefixes mean "no" or "not":

      un-   in-   im-   dis-

C. Change each of the following words to its opposite meaning by using one of the preceding prefixes. Use your dictionary if necessary.

1.	*un*	happy	9.	____	satisfied
2.	____	married	10.	____	pleasant
3.	____	natural	11.	____	advantage
4.	____	possible	12.	____	similar
5.	*dis*	content	13.	____	fortunate
6.	____	equal	14.	____	appear
7.	____	healthful	15.	____	honest
8.	____	known	16.	____	polite

Study Skill: Finding Reading Clues

Read the following selection carefully.

A Murder Mystery (continued)

Y   "Why did I hate my husband?" Mrs. Pennwright repeated. "He had a terrible personality. We were always arguing because we had nothing in common. I wanted to see a marriage counselor, but he wouldn't even talk about it."

Z   "He drank too much alcohol, and he had a drinking problem. Because of his job, he was always eating. He became terribly fat. Yes, I hated him."

AA   She stared straight into Grimsley's eyes. "However," she said, "I did not kill him. When I last saw him, he was eating some cheese, drinking some wine, and reading a magazine. I left the hotel room and was watching TV and talking with Mr. Goodbody in the bar all evening. Then Mr. Welles ran in and told us about Ambrose."

BB   "Aha!" said Grimsley. "You found the body, Mr. Welles?"

CC   "Yes," Welles said. "I was walking past the Pennwrights' room when I heard a low voice inside: Someone needed help! The door was locked. After I tried for about five minutes to open it, I finally broke down the door. Unfortunately, I was too late. There was Ambrose on the floor— dead. He was lying on top of his magazine. I ran to the hotel manager, and he went to you. Then I went into the bar, told Mrs. Pennwright and Mr. Goodbody about the murder, and we came to this office."

DD   "Hmmmm . . . ." Grimsley walked slowly back and forth for several minutes. Then he stopped.

EE   "Aha!" he finally shouted. "I know the answer to this mystery—the murderer and the murder weapon! I am quite sure that . . ."

What did Detective Grimsley know? Complete the following exercises and you will find the answers! A good reader is like a good detective: He or she looks for clues (pieces of information that lead to an answer). Pretend you are a detective when you do these exercises.

1. Go back to the beginning of the chapter and look carefully at the picture again. Then reread paragraph G of the reading selection on page 75. On the lines here, list *all* possible clues. (Some might be helpful; some might not be.)

    _____

    _____

    _____

    _____

2. Now reread paragraphs AA and CC of the reading on page 84 carefully and check your list in item 1 above. What is in Mrs. Pennwright's and Mr. Welles' stories that is not in the picture?

    _____

    What is in the picture that is not in their stories?

    _____

3. When two ideas are *contradictory,* one idea has to be false if the other is true. Often in a mystery story, one or more suspects are lying (not telling the truth). Is any suspect here lying? If so, who is lying, and what are the lies? Look at the picture at the beginning of the chapter. Then reread paragraphs C on page 74 and CC on page 84 for contradictory information.

    _____

    _____

4. Reread paragraphs G on page 75 and M on page 80. Which two facts might go together?

    _____

    _____

5. According to the preceding clues, what was the murder weapon?

    _____

    Who was the murderer? How do you know? _____

    _____

The answer to the mystery is at the end of the chapter.

PART FOUR

SCANNING FOR INFORMATION

The front of most telephone books contains information about emergencies. You will not understand all the words, and there isn't time in an emergency to look in a dictionary. Figure out the meaning from *clues* in the context and the pictures.

Look at the following section from the telephone book. Read the questions about the selection, and find the information as fast as you can. Write the answers on the lines.

Here are some important words:

> poison = something that can kill people if they eat or drink it
> swallow = to take through the mouth into the stomach
> victim = the person who dies or is hurt
> unconscious = not awake
> vomit = to bring something up from the stomach through the mouth
> roll = turn
> choke = to be unable to breathe because something is in the throat

1. What are some examples of poisons? _____

    _____

2. Who are most often the victims of poisoning? _____

3. What are the two important words in step 1? What do they mean? _____

    _____

4. What is the first necessary action in case of poisoning?

    _____

5. What two places can you call for help in case of poisoning?

    _____

    Complete the following sentences or answer the questions:

6. If the patient (victim) is unconscious, you need to find out if he or she is

    _____.

    If not, you have to _____

    _____ and

    _____

7. Can you give an unconscious victim water? _____

POISONING

The home is loaded with poisons: Cosmetics, Detergents, Bleaches, Cleaning Solutions, Glue, Lye, Paint, Turpentine, Kerosene, Gasoline and other petroleum products, Alcohol, Aspirin and other medications, and on and on.

1. **Small children are most often the victims of accidental poisoning. If a child has swallowed or is suspected to have swallowed any substance that might be poisonous, assume the worst — TAKE ACTION.**

2. **Call your Poison Control Center. If none is in your area, call your emergency medical rescue squad. Bring suspected item and container with you.**

3. **What you can do if the victim is unconscious:**

   A. Make sure patient is breathing. If not, tilt head back and perform mouth to mouth breathing. Do not give anything by mouth. Do not attempt to stimulate person. Call emergency rescue squad immediately.

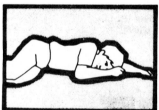

4. **If the victim is vomiting:**

   A. Roll him or her over onto the left side so that the person will not choke on what is brought up.

5. **Be prepared. Determine and verify your Poison Control Center and Fire Department Rescue Squad numbers and keep them near your telephone.**

8. If the patient is vomiting, you should _____

   _____.

   Why? _____

9. How can you be prepared for an emergency (poisoning)?

   _____

Going Beyond the Text

Find the telephone numbers of the Poison Control Center and the Fire Department Rescue Squad Number in your local telephone book. Write them here: _____

_____

Write other emergency telephone numbers here:

_____   _____

_____   _____

_____   _____

Skim the information in the front of your telephone book about other emergencies. Summarize the information for the class.

PERSONAL STORIES

Follow these steps for the stories:

1. Read them quickly and tell the main ideas.
2. Answer your instructor's questions about the stories, or ask and answer questions of your own.
3. Tell your own opinions of the ideas in the stories.
4. Tell or write about emergencies in your own life.

Emergencies: Two Stories

A   I live in California, and we have earthquakes here all the time. Sometimes they're strong. Things fall off shelves, and windows break. It's well known that a very big earthquake will probably hit this area in the near future. Everyone is preparing for it. Some people are terribly afraid. But usually we have small earthquakes. Sometimes we don't even notice them. For example, one evening I was sitting outside, on the patio. The ground began to shake very gently. At first, I wasn't sure it was an earthquake. It felt like I was in the water—in a swimming pool or a lake—with the water moving gently under me. I know this sounds crazy, but it was almost relaxing. I felt calm. Perhaps because of this experience, I'm not as worried about earthquakes as I used to be.

B   Once, when I was a kid, I was on vacation with my father. We were driving to a national forest in the mountains. We had to cross a very hot, dry desert on our way to the mountains. Our car didn't have air conditioning, and the temperature was over 110 degrees. Every five or ten minutes I asked, "Are we almost there?" My father always said, "No. A few more hours." Then the most terrible thing happened. Our car broke down. It simply stopped there in the desert. We were a hundred miles from houses, gas stations, or people. We were hot, thirsty, and tired. I was very afraid. "We're going to die!" I said. (I was thinking of old movies on TV. People in old movies always die in the desert.) "We're not going to die," my father said. "Yes we are," I said. "There's nobody to help us. After two weeks the police will find our bodies, and . . ." Just then a car came by and stopped. "Need some help?" the driver asked. My father smiled at me. "You watch too much TV, kid," he said.

Answer to the Mystery: The murder weapon was the caviar, and Gregory Welles was the murderer. He had the caviar with him from his gourmet restaurant. There was no caviar in their hotel room when Althea Pennwright left her husband. Welles brought Ambrose poisoned caviar. He knew that Ambrose was reading a magazine because he saw him alive. (The magazine was not visible under Ambrose's fat, dead body.) Also, Welles was lying when he said that he heard Ambrose's low voice from his hotel room because the wind outside was very loud. Ambrose loved food, so he ate all the caviar; then he died. Then Welles broke down the door and went to the hotel manager.

7

HEALTH AND ILLNESS

THE SECRETS OF A VERY LONG LIFE

Getting Started

Look at the picture and talk about it.

1. Where does it take place? Who are the two people? What are they doing?
2. Describe the lifestyle of the old couple. What do they probably do all day? What do they probably eat?
3. Do you know any very old people? How is their lifestyle similar to the lifestyle of the people in the picture? How is it different?

Preparing to Read

Think about the answers to these questions. (The reading selection will answer them.)

1. What places in the world are famous for people who live a very long time?
2. Describe the environment in these places.
3. What kind of diet do people in these places have?
4. What might be some secrets of long life?

Glancing at Vocabulary (optional)

Here are some vocabulary items from the reading selection. You can learn them now or come back to them later.

Nouns	Verb	Adjectives	Expression
world	solve	modern	not only . . . but also
area		physical	
secret		simple	
eyesight		amazing	
exercise		surprising	
worry		natural	

Read the following selection quickly. Then answer the questions after the reading.

The Secrets of a Very Long Life

A   There are several places in the world that are famous for people who live a very long time. These places are usually in mountainous areas, far away from modern cities. Doctors, scientists, and public health experts often travel to these regions to solve the mystery of a long, healthy life; the experts hope to bring to the modern world the secrets of longevity.

B   Hunza is high in the Himalayan Mountains of Asia. There, many people over one hundred years of age are still in good physical health. Men of ninety are new fathers, and women of fifty still have babies. What are the reasons for this good health? Scientists believe that the people of Hunza have these three benefits: (1) physical work, usually in the fields or with animals; (2) a healthful environment with clean air and water; and (3) a simple diet high in vitamins and nutrition but low in fat, cholesterol, sugar, and chemicals.

C   People in the Caucasus Mountains in the Soviet Union are also famous for their longevity. In this area, there are amazing examples of very long-lived people. Although birth records are not usually available, a woman called Tsurba probably lived until age 160; a man called Shirali may have lived until age 168. His widow was 120 years old. In general, the people not only live a long time, but they also live *well*. They are almost never sick, and when they die, they have not only their own teeth but also a full head of hair, and good eyesight.

D   Vilcabamba, Ecuador, is another area famous for the longevity of its inhabitants. This region—like Hunza and the Caucasus—is also in high mountains, far away from cities. In Vilcabamba, too, there is very little serious disease. One reason for the good health of the people might be the clean, beautiful environment: The temperature is about 70° Fahrenheit all year long; the wind always comes from the same direction; and the region is rich in flowers, fruit, vegetables, and wildlife.

E   In some ways, the diets of the inhabitants in the three regions are quite different. Hunzukuts eat mainly raw vegetables, fruit (especially apricots) and *chapatis*—a kind of pancake; they eat meat only a few times a year. The Caucasan diet consists mainly of milk, cheese, vegetables, fruit, and meat; most people there drink the local red wine daily. In Vilcabamba, people eat a small amount of meat each week, but the diet consists largely of grain, corn, beans, potatoes, and fruit.

F   Experts found one surprising fact in the mountains of Ecuador: Most people there, even the very old, consume a lot of coffee, drink large amounts of alcohol, and smoke forty to sixty cigarettes daily!

G   However, the diets are similar in two general ways: (1) the fruits and vegetables that the inhabitants of the three areas eat are all natural; that is, they contain no chemicals; and (2) the people consume fewer calories than people do in other parts of the world. A typical North American takes in an average of 3,300 calories every day; a typical inhabitant of these mountainous areas, between 1,700 and 2,000 calories.

H   Inhabitants in the three regions have more in common than calories, natural food, their mountains, and their distance from modern cities. Because these people live in the countryside and are mostly farmers, their lives are physically hard. Thus, they do not need to go to health clubs because they get a lot of exercise in their daily work. In addition, although their lives are hard, the people do not seem to have the worries of city people. Their lives are quiet. Consequently, some experts believe that physical exercise and freedom from worry might be the two most important secrets of longevity.

Getting the Main Ideas

Write T (true) or F (false) on the lines.

1. _____   Doctors and scientists study certain people to learn their secrets of long life.

2. _____   The areas of the world where people live a very long time are usually near the sea, and the weather is very hot.

3. _____   There is one main reason for the good health and long lives of these people.

4. _____   According to experts, most people in these regions eat mainly junk food, drink a lot of alcohol, and smoke cigarettes.

5. _____   The secrets of long life might be lots of rest and no hard work.

Guessing Meaning from Context

The questions after each of the following sentences will lead you to clues to the meaning of the underlined words. Find the answers and write them on the lines. Then circle the letter of the words that give the correct meaning of the underlined vocabulary items.

1. Doctors, scientists, and public health <u>experts</u> often travel to these places to study the causes of a long, healthy life.

   Who studies the reasons for a long, healthy life? _____

   _____

   Do doctors and scientists know about public health? _____

   Are doctors and scientists experts? _____

   What are *experts*?

   a. people who live a long time
   b. people who know a lot about a subject

   c. students
   d. travelers to many regions of the world

2. Scientists believe that the people of Hunza have the benefit of a healthful <u>environment</u> with clean air and water.

   What are two things that an environment can have? _____

   _____

   Where is the environment? _____

   What is an *environment*?

   a. clean air and water
   b. a healthful place

   c. a place in Hunza for scientists
   d. the conditions in a place that influence people

3. In this area, there are examples of very <u>long-lived</u> people. A woman called Tsurba, for instance, lived until age 160.

   Did Tsurba live a long time? _____

   What is Tsurba an example of? _____

   What does *long-lived* mean?

   a. having a long life
   b. being 160 years old

   c. living in one place for years
   d. being an example

Which words in each of the following sentences give clues to the meanings of the underlined words? Circle them. Then circle the letters of the words that give the correct meanings of the underlined vocabulary items.

4. People in the Caucasus Mountains in the Soviet Union are also famous for their <u>longevity</u>. In this <u>mountainous</u> area, the people not only live a long time, but they also live well.

   mountainous:

   a. in the Caucasus
   b. in the Soviet Union
   c. having mountains
   d. famous

   longevity:

   a. long length of life
   b. a long time
   c. the environment of the mountains
   d. health

5. Vilcabamba, Ecuador, is another area famous for the longevity of its <u>inhabitants</u>. One reason for the health of the people in this <u>region</u> might be the clean, beautiful environment.

   inhabitants:

   a. the people of an area
   b. cities
   c. the environment
   d. Ecuadorians

   region:

   a. Ecuador
   b. area
   c. healthy place
   d. beauty

6. Most people there <u>consume</u> a lot of coffee and drink large amounts of alcohol. A typical North American consumes an average of 3,300 calories a day.

   consume:

   a. drink but not eat
   b. take in
   c. average
   d. have a lot of calories

Recognizing Reading Structure

Many reading selections follow an "outline." The outline is the plan of the material; it shows the relationship of the topics and ideas. The general parts of a main topic appear below it, and sometimes each part has details.

Example: Reasons for Good Health of the Hunzukuts

    1. Physical work

        a. In the fields
        b. With animals

    2. A healthy environment

        a. Clean air
        b. Clean water

    3. A simple diet

        a. High in vitamins
        b. Low in fat
        c. Low in sugar
        d. Without chemicals

A. On the lines, answer the following questions about the sample outline.

1. What is the one main topic of the outline? _____

2. How many general reasons are there for the good health of the people of

    Hunza? _____ What are the reasons? _____

    _____

3. What two kinds of physical work do the Hunzukuts do? _____

    _____

4. What are two characteristics of a healthy environment? _____

    _____

5. How many characteristics of a simple diet are there in the outline? _____

B. On the lines, write the missing points in the following outline, according to the reading selection. In the parentheses, write the letter of the paragraph that tells about that topic.

THE SECRETS OF A VERY LONG LIFE

1. Places where people live a long time

    a. Hunza (in the Himalayan Mountains)   ( )

    b. _____ ( )

    c. _____ ( )

2. Diets of the three regions

    a. Differences   ( )

       (1) _____

       (2) Food in the Caucasus

       (3) _____

    b. Similarities   ( )

       (1) Natural food

       (2) _____

3. Other causes of long life

    a. Hard physical work   ( )

    b. _____

C. Now circle the number of the one main idea of the reading.

1. There are several places in the world where people live a long time.
2. The secrets of longevity may be diet, physical activity, and freedom from worry.
3. In the Caucasus Mountains, people live even longer than people in Ecuador.
4. The inhabitants of mountain regions usually eat healthful foods.

Understanding Details

Punctuation often provides clues to the meaning of sentences and paragraphs. A colon (:) can introduce a list that explains the sentence before the colon. Sometimes each item of the list has a number before it. Commas separate the items. (If one or more items contain commas themselves, semicolons often separate the items.)

Example: The old people of the area live well: (1) they are rarely sick; and (2) when they die, they have their own teeth, a full head of hair, and good eyesight. (What do the two numbered items show? Examples of how the old people live well.)

A. Find the answer to each of the following questions about the reading selection. Write the answers on the lines.

1. According to scientists, what are the three reasons for the good health of the people of Hunza?

    a. _____

    b. _____

    c. _____

2. What are the characteristics of the environment in Vilcabamba, Ecuador? _____

    _____

    _____

3. How are the diets of the inhabitants of Hunza, the Caucasus, and Vilcabamba

    similar? _____

    _____

Sometimes a writer leaves words out of a sentence because the reader already knows them from other parts of the sentence.

Example: The Hunzukuts eat mainly raw fruits and vegetables; the people of the Caucasus, mainly milk and meat. (The word *eat* is missing before *mainly milk and meat* because it appears in the first part of the sentence.)

B. Find the answer to each of the following questions about the reading selection. Write the answers on the lines.

1. How old were the two Hunzukuts in the reading (Tsurba and Shirali) when they died? _____

2. How many calories a day do the people of these three mountain regions consume? _____

Now turn back to the "Preparing to Read" section on page 91 and answer the questions.

Discussing the Reading

Talk about your answers to the following questions.

1. Are there any places in your country with groups of people famous for their longevity?
2. Are the old people you know healthy? Do they have any "secrets" to long life? Can you suggest any other things that might lead to a long, healthy old age?
3. How is your life similar to the lives of the people in these three regions? How is it different?
4. Do you hope to live a very long life? What will your lifestyle probably be if you live to be one hundred years old?

PART TWO

DISEASE DETECTIVES

Glancing at Vocabulary (optional)

Here are some vocabulary items from the next reading selection. You can learn them now or come back to them later.

Nouns			Verbs	Adjectives	Adverbs
medicine	drug	accident	fight	recent	moreover
technology	dirt	microscope	accept	exciting	previously
transplant	plant	computer		successful	
organ	laboratory	patient			

Skimming for Main Ideas

Read the selection on the following page quickly. Then circle the number of the one main idea of each section.

Disease Detectives

A   Two recent changes are making modern medicine a more popular and exciting field of study than ever before. First, new technology is now available to modern "disease detectives," doctors and scientists who are putting together clues to solve medical mysteries—that is, to find out the answers to questions of health and sickness. Also, transplants of the heart, liver, kidney, and other organs of the body are much more common than they were ten or twenty years ago.

1. Organ transplants are very common now.
2. Two recent changes make modern medicine exciting.
3. Disease detectives can solve medical mysteries.

B   Modern "disease detectives" are microbiologists, epidemiologists, and other scientists who try to find out the reason for an epidemic—a sickness that many people in one region have. These experts talk to people who have the disease and ask many questions, such as: What do you eat most often? How often do you wash your hands? Do you use drugs? They examine kitchens, bathrooms, and air conditioning systems. Then they study the outside environment—dirt, plants, rivers and lakes, areas for animals, and so on—for clues that might give them information about disease. They share the information that they find with laboratory scientists who have the benefits of microscopes and computers. Together, these disease detectives work to find the causes of modern killer diseases.

1. Modern "disease detectives" are doctors.
2. Several kinds of scientists do many things to find out the causes of diseases.
3. Microbiologists study the indoor and outdoor environment.

C   Organ transplants are common today. Because of modern technology, moreover, they are more successful than they were in the past; in other words, people with a new heart, liver, or kidney can live much longer than they did previously. Not long ago, transplant patients often died after a few days because their bodies fought against the new organ. A new drug, however, now helps the human body accept its new part.

1. In the past, people did not live very long after receiving organ transplants.
2. Heart and liver transplants are dangerous because the human body fights against a new organ.
3. Because of modern medical science, organ transplants are now more successful than ever before.

Viewpoint

In many reading selections, the authors tell or imply (suggest) their opinions about the topic. What is the viewpoint of the author of the second reading selection in this chapter? Circle one of the choices in parentheses.

1. The author (believes / does not believe) in the use of modern technology to solve health problems.
2. She thinks that new developments in medicine are (good / bad) for people.

Discussing the Reading

Talk about your answers to the following questions:

1. What are some examples of modern epidemics in your country? What are some in the United States and Canada? Do doctors or scientists know the reasons for these epidemics? Do they have any ideas about the cures?
2. Do you know anyone with a transplanted organ? Do you think that organ transplants are a good idea? What are some possible difficulties with or objections to them?

PART THREE

BUILDING VOCABULARY; STUDY SKILLS

A. Without a dictionary, match the words with similar meanings. Write the correct letter on the line.

1. __e__ longevity
2. _____ region
3. _____ consume
4. _____ receive
5. _____ cause
6. _____ technology

a. area
b. reason
c. science
d. eat or drink
e. long life
f. accept

B. Fill in the blanks. Choose from the following words to complete the sentences. Use each word one time.

microscopes	diet	inhabitants	secrets	raw
mountainous	experts	computers	freedom	physical

1. The ___*secrets*___ of longevity may come to us from _____ regions of the world, far away from modern cities.

2. The _____ of the _____ of these regions usually includes _____ fruits and vegetables.

3. Some _____ believe that _____ exercise and _____ from worry are two reasons for long life.

4. With _____ and _____ , laboratory scientists try to find out the reasons for an epidemic.

Study Skill: Recognizing Paraphrases

> To understand and remember information in a reading, it often helps to "para-phrase" it—that is, to say it another way.
>
> *Example:* Two recent changes are making modern medicine a more popular and exciting field of study than ever before. (This sentence means: "Medicine is more exciting now than it used to be because of two recent changes, so more people want to study it.")

For each of the following items, circle the letter of the paraphrase (the sentence with a similar meaning).

1. Fortunately, new technology is now available to modern "disease detectives" who are putting together clues to solve medical mysteries.

    a. Modern science helps "disease detectives" answer the questions of medicine.
    b. We are fortunate to have technology in medicine.
    c. Detectives need new clues to solve the mysteries of sick people.

2. Transplants of the heart, liver, kidney, and other organs of the body are much more common than they were ten or twenty years ago.

    a. Transplants of body organs were not common ten years ago.
    b. The heart, the liver, and the kidney are organs; doctors transplant them from one body to another much more often now than previously.

   c.   People with organ transplants are much healthier than people who lived twenty years ago.

3.   Because of modern technology, organ transplants are more successful today than they were in the past. Not long ago, transplant patients often died after a few days because their bodies fought against the new organ. A new drug, however, now helps the human body accept its new part.

   a.   Organ transplants were not successful in the past because doctors did not give their patients drugs.

   b.   Today, patients never die after an organ transplant because their bodies accept it.

   c.   With a new drug, organ transplants succeed more often because the patient's body does not fight against the new organ.

PART FOUR

SCANNING FOR INFORMATION

It is important to be able to follow directions on medicine labels. Look at the following labels and then read the questions on page 105. Find the information as fast as you can. Write the answers on the lines.

Here are some words from medicine labels:

prescription = doctor's directions for medicine

as directed = the way that the doctor said

capsule, tablet = kinds of pills

discard = throw away

dosage = amount that you should take

drowsiness = sleepiness

exp. (or expir.) = expiration date (do not use the drug after this date)

orally = by mouth

soothe = to make something feel better

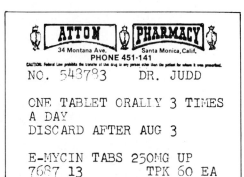

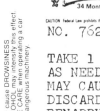

ATTON PHARMACY
34 Montana Ave.   Santa Monica, Calif.
PHONE 451-141

CAUTION Federal Law prohibits the transfer of this drug to any person other than the patient for whom it was prescribed.

NO. 762781   DR. DAVIS

TAKE 1 CAPSULE 3 TIMES DAILY
AS NEEDED FOR ITCHING.
MAY CAUSE DROWSINESS
DISCARD AFTER 9/94
BENADRYL CAPS 25MG PD
67487   4SEP83   TPK 30 EA

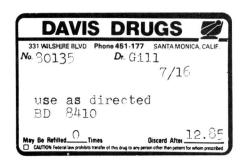

DAVIS DRUGS
331 WILSHIRE BLVD   Phone 451-177   SANTA MONICA, CALIF.
No. 30135   Dr. Gill
                        7/16

use as directed
BD   8410

May Be Refilled __0__ Times   Discard After __12.85__

ATTON PHARMACY
34 Montana Ave.   Santa Monica, Calif.
PHONE 451-141

CAUTION Federal Law prohibits the transfer of this drug to any person other than the patient for whom it was prescribed.

NO. 468492W   DR. MYERS

ONE TABLET DAILY WITH
BANANA AND 1 GLASS OF
ORANGE JUICE.
DISCARD AFTER 6/94.

FUROSEMIDE TABS 40MG SEARL
78498 26 May 83   KHN 10 EA

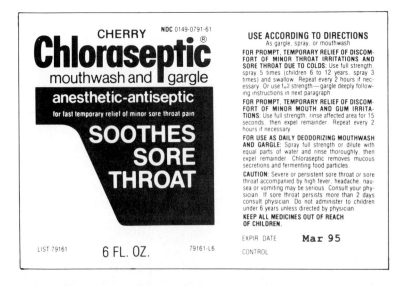

1. Which two drugs can you buy in the drugstore without a prescription? _____

_____

2. What are the names of the prescription drugs? _____

_____

3. Which medicine is for a sore throat? _____

Which is for itching of the skin? _____

Which is for headaches and other pains? _____

4. According to the doctor, how often should the patient take a Benadryl capsule?

_____

How many tablets should the patient take? _____

5. How many Bayer aspirin tablets can a patient take at one time? _____

How often can the patient take aspirin? _____

6. How do people use Chloraseptic? _____

_____

7. How much medicine is there in a bottle of Bayer aspirin? _____

_____

How much is there in a bottle of Chloraseptic? _____

_____

8. What is today's date? _____

Can a patient take E-Mycin today? _____

What is the expiration date of Benadryl? _____

9. What are the side effects (the things that might happen to a patient) of Benadryl?

_____

10. What warning appears on most medicine labels? _____

_____

Going Beyond the Text

Bring some medicine containers or some ads for drugstore medicine to class. List the new words and abbreviations. Find out their meanings.

Read some of the items aloud. Decide which medicines are for which sicknesses or health problems (headaches, sore throats, colds, skin problems, etc.).

Discuss medicines. When should a patient take them? For how long? Is medicine always good for people? Why or why not?

PART FIVE

PERSONAL STORIES

Follow these steps in the story:

1. Read it quickly and tell the main idea.
2. Answer your instructor's questions about the story, or ask and answer questions of your own.
3. Tell your own opinions of the ideas in the story.
4. Tell or write about a problem of your own with health.

Up in Smoke

A   I began to smoke in high school. My friends smoked. My parents smoked. It seemed to be a natural, "adult" thing to do. But forty years later we all started to hear about the effects of cigarette smoke: lung disease, cancer, and heart problems. I didn't pay much attention to these reports. I felt healthy, and I thought I was taking good care of myself.

B   Then two things happened. First, I started to cough. I thought it was just a cold, but it didn't get better. Second, my brother got lung cancer. He got sicker and sicker. He died last year. My brother and I smoked our first cigarettes together over forty years ago, and we smoked our last cigarettes together eleven months ago. I sat with him in his hospital room, and I decided to quit. No more cigarettes, I told myself.

C   However, it was very hard to quit, although I knew I ought to. Nicotine is a drug; as a result, cigarettes cause a powerful addiction. I tried several times to quit, but I couldn't. Then I tried the "Stop Smoking" program at a hospital. It wasn't easy. For the first two months I thought about cigarettes all the time. I didn't sleep well. I ate a lot and gained ten pounds. I was nervous, and my hands shook. I became angry very easily—not only at important things but also small ones. The effect of the nicotine was amazing.

D   I very slowly started to lose my need for cigarettes. My cough disappeared. Sleep wasn't a problem anymore. I became calmer. And when I exercised, I had more energy. I feel better now. I don't always think about cigarettes, but I *do* feel the need for one five or six times every day. I hope my grandchildren keep themselves healthy; they had better not start to smoke. It's a terrible addiction.

8

TELEVISION AND THE MEDIA

TELEVISION: HOW IT AFFECTS US

Getting Started

Look at the pictures and talk about them.

1. What are the people doing?
2. How are the two groups of people different? How are their TV programs different?

Preparing to Read

Think about the answers to these questions. (The reading selection will answer them.)

1. In what ways is TV good?
2. What effects does TV have on the human brain?
3. How does TV cause us to be dissatisfied?
4. What effect does TV violence have on many people?
5. What are the signs of TV addiction?

Glancing at Vocabulary (optional)

Here are some vocabulary items from the reading selection. You can learn them now or come back to them later.

Nouns	Verbs	Expressions
the arts	affect	as well as
brain	benefit	pay attention
actor	cut	fall asleep
film		real life
dependence	**Adjectives**	take a break
scissors	clear	
cord	negative	
	lazy	

Read the following selection. Then answer the questions after the reading.

Television: How It Affects Us

A How does television affect our lives? It can be very helpful to people who carefully choose the shows that they watch. Television can increase our knowledge of the outside world; there are high-quality programs that help us understand many fields of study: science, medicine, the arts, and so on. Moreover, television benefits very old people who can't often leave the house, as well as patients in hospitals. It also offers nonnative speakers the advantage of daily informal language practice; they can increase their vocabulary and practice listening.

B On the other hand, there are several serious disadvantages to television. Of course, it provides us with a pleasant way to relax and spend our free time, but in some countries, people watch the "boob tube" for an average of six hours or more a day. Many children stare at a TV screen for more hours each day than they do anything else, including studying and sleeping. It's clear that the tube has a powerful influence on their lives and that its influence is often negative.

C Recent studies show that after only thirty seconds of TV, a person's brain "relaxes" the same way that it does just before the person falls asleep. Another effect of television on the human brain is that it seems to cause poor concentration. Children who view a lot of TV can often concentrate on a subject for only fifteen to twenty minutes; they can pay attention only for the amount of time between commercials!

D Another disadvantage is that TV often causes people to become dissatisfied with their own lives. Real life does not seem as exciting to these people as the lives of actors on the screen. To many people, TV becomes more real than reality, and their own lives seem boring. Also, many people get upset or depressed when they can't solve problems in real life as quickly as TV actors seem to. On the screen, actors solve serious problems in a half-hour program or a thirty-second commercial.

E   Before a child is fourteen years old, he or she views eleven thousand murders on the tube. He or she begins to believe that there is nothing strange about fights, killings, and other kinds of violence. Many studies show that people become more violent after certain programs. They may even do the things that they saw in a violent show. An example is the effect of the movie *The Deer Hunter*. After it appeared on TV in the United States, twenty-nine people tried to kill themselves in a way similar to an event in the film.

F   The most negative effect of the "boob tube" might be people's addiction to it. People often feel a strange and powerful need to watch TV even when they don't enjoy it. Addiction to a TV screen is similar to drug or alcohol addiction: People almost never believe they are addicted. Answer these questions about your television habits:

1. Do you come home from school or work and immediately turn on the TV set?
2. Do you watch more than ten hours of TV a week?
3. Can you concentrate for only fifteen to twenty minutes before you need to take a break?
4. Do you feel closer to actors on the screen than to real people in your own life?
5. Do you feel lazy and sleepy when you watch TV programs?
6. Do you believe that the products that you see on commercials can make you happier?
7. Are you dissatisfied with your life because it isn't exciting?

If you answered "yes" to these questions, you probably have a TV addiction! The "cure" is to throw away the set, or to take some scissors and cut the cord.

Getting the Main Ideas

Write T (true) or F (false) on the lines.

1. _____   The effects of TV on our lives are always negative.

2. _____   Television affects the human brain.

3. _____   The lives of people who watch a lot of television seem very exciting.

4. _____   The violence on TV influences people.

5. _____   Some people need to watch television; they don't feel good without it.

Guessing Meaning from Context

Circle the words in each of the following sentences that give clues to the meaning of the underlined vocabulary item. Then circle the letter of the word that gives the correct meaning of the item.

1. Television can increase our knowledge of the outside world; there are many high-quality programs that help us understand many fields of study: science, medicine, the arts, and so on.

    a. life   b. understanding   c. size

2. Children who view a lot of TV can often concentrate on a subject for only fifteen to twenty minutes; they can pay attention only for the amount of time between TV commercials!

    view: a. watch   b. enjoy   c. need

    concentrate: a. enjoy   b. understand   c. pay attention

3. To many people, television becomes more real than reality, and their own lives seem boring because they are not as exciting as the lives of actors on TV.

    reality: a. real life   b. programs   c. the present moment

    boring: a. exciting   b. not interesting   c. worried

4. A child begins to believe there is nothing strange about fights, killings, and other kinds of violence.

    a. mysteries that detectives can't solve
    b. actions that hurt people physically
    c. arguments between people

5. The most negative effect of television might be some people's strong addiction to it. They feel a strange and powerful need to watch it even when they don't enjoy it.

    a. enjoyment of   b. dislike of   c. need for

6. Addiction to TV is similar to drug or alcohol dependence: People almost never believe they are addicted. The "cure" is to throw away the TV—or to cut the cord with scissors.

    addicted: a. intelligent   b. dependent   c. dissatisfied

    cure: a. solution   b. disease   c. reality

7. Do you believe that your life will be more exciting and happier if you buy the <u>products</u> that you see on TV <u>commercials</u>?

products:

a. drugs or alcohol   b. things for sale   c. benefits

commercials:

a. exciting shows   b. violent movies   c. breaks in the programs

Recognizing Reading Structure

A. Circle the number of the *one* main idea of the reading.

1. Television teaches us about science, medicine, and the arts.
2. Television has several negative effects on people.
3. Television causes people to be violent.
4. Many people are addicted to television.

Sometimes a reading selection follows an outline. The outline shows the organization of the topics and ideas in the reading.

B. Put the following topics in the right places in the outline that follows. The letters in parentheses after the lines show the letters of the paragraphs that tell about the topics.

The effect of TV on the brain

The influence of TV violence on people

The amount of time some people
   watch TV

The positive effects of TV

Television addiction, its signs, and its
   cure

The comparison of TV programs to
   real life

TELEVISION: HOW IT AFFECTS US

I. _____ (A)

II. Disadvantages of TV

    A. *The amount of time some people watch TV* (B)

    B. _____ (C)

    C. _____ (D)

    D. _____ (E)

    E. _____ (F)

C. Which of the following details belong to which topics? In the parentheses, write the letter of the topic from the outline. Then turn back to the reading to check your answers.

1. (   ) A person's brain relaxes when he or she watches TV.
2. (   ) You can solve the problem of TV addiction if you throw away the set.
3. (   ) Some people watch television for more than six hours a day.
4. (   ) Children aren't upset by violence because they see it all the time on TV.
5. (   ) Many people are addicted to TV.
6. (   ) Many children spend most of their time in front of the TV.
7. (   ) Television isn't good for concentration.
8. (   ) There are seven signs of TV addiction.
9. (   ) Some people do the violent things they see on TV.
10. (   ) Television offers high-quality programs on different subjects.
11. (   ) Nonnative speakers can improve their English by watching TV.
12. (   ) Because of exciting TV programs, some people become depressed or upset about their own lives.
13. (   ) Television helps people who can't move around a lot.

Understanding Details

Circle the letters of *all* the correct phrases for each number and write the letters in the following blanks. For help, refer to the reading on pages 110–111.

1. Television _____.

   a. can teach us about many subjects
   b. helps ESL students to learn English
   c. is better for children than for very old people
   d. increases our powers of concentration

2. Many people who watch a lot of TV _____.

   a. cannot usually relax
   b. become dissatisfied with the reality of their own lives
   c. can solve their problems more quickly
   d. take scissors and cut the TV cord

3. Violence on TV _____.

   a. may cause people to act violently
   b. is not very bad
   c. includes fights and murders
   d. affects only children

4. One "sign" of TV addiction is _____.

   a. a set that you have on for more than one hour a day
   b. the need to turn on the set as soon as you come home
   c. a feeling of closeness to TV actors
   d. sleepiness when you see commercials but not movies

Now turn back to the "Preparing to Read" section on page 109 and answer the questions.

Discussing the Reading

Talk about your answers to the following questions.

1. Do you have a television set? How many hours do you watch it every day?
2. Which shows do you like most? Why?
3. Which shows don't you like? Why?
4. Does TV help you in any way? If so, how?
5. Go back to the reading (page 111) and read about the signs of addiction again. Are you addicted to TV? If so, which signs of addiction do you have? Do you know anyone who is addicted to television? Which signs does he or she have?

PART TWO

A CASE STUDY

Glancing at Vocabulary (optional)

Here are some vocabulary items from the next reading selection. You can learn them now or come back to them later.

Nouns	Verbs	Expression
sofa	reply	be in love with
symptom	hide	
boyfriend		
toothpaste	Conjunction	
shampoo	although	
jeans		
trouble		

Skimming for Main Ideas

Read the following selection as fast as you can.

A Case Study

A patient went into her doctor's office. She lay down on his sofa. The doctor sat in a large chair and opened his notebook.

"Oh, Dr. Brainstorm," she said sadly, "I'm so unhappy. What's wrong with me?"

"I don't know," he replied. "What are your symptoms?"

"Well," she began, "I'm not really sick, but I'm just so depressed all the time! My daily life is terribly boring. Although I do everything right, I'm not very popular, and I don't have any boyfriends."

"What do you mean, 'do everything right'?" asked the doctor.

"Oh, you know. I use Everwhite toothpaste and Perfect Shine shampoo. I wear Lovely Lady makeup and Extremely Slinky jeans. But nobody seems to like me. I can't understand it. I'm so confused!"

"Hmmm. I see," said Dr. Brainstorm. "What else is worrying you?"

"My life isn't the same as other people's. I think there's something terribly wrong with me."

"What do other people do?"

"Well, Alicia, for example, is married to a successful microbiologist, but she's secretly in love with a computer expert whom she met at a health club. This computer expert, Max, still has a wife, a laboratory scientist, who is hiding on a mountainous island in the Caribbean because she killed a young man in a car accident four years ago. She's afraid that the police will find out and look for her. Alicia and Max don't know that the young man was actually Alicia's brother, a foreign student at a college in the Midwest."

"Amazing!" said Dr. Brainstorm. "How much time do you spend with these friends of yours?"

"Oh, about four hours a day."

"And how is your life different from theirs?"

"I just go to work, come home, watch TV, and go to bed. Nothing exciting ever happens to me."

" I see," said the doctor. "I think I know your trouble. You have a fairly common problem with reality. However, I know exactly how to solve it."

Dr. Brainstorm opened a desk drawer, took out a pair of scissors, and gave them to his patient.

Inferring: Figuring Out the Meaning

A reading selection gives information from which a reader can often infer (figure out) other information. In this story, the writer only implies the main idea; that is, she leads the reader to the main idea, but she does not express it in words.

Look back at the reading selection to find clues to the answers to the following questions. Write the answers on the lines. The answers will help you figure out the main idea.

1. Does Dr. Brainstorm try to cure patients' physical diseases or their personal

    problems? _____

    How do you know this? _____

2. What does the patient do to be popular and find boyfriends? _____

    _____

    _____

3. In your opinion, where did the patient find out about Everwhite toothpaste,

    Extremely Slinky jeans, and so on? _____

4. In your opinion, who are the people that the patient discusses (Alicia, Max, and

    so on) in real life? _____

5. Reread the list on page 111. What are five clues to the patient's problem? _____

    _____

    _____

6. What is the patient's problem? _____

7. What does the doctor want her to do with the scissors? _____

    _____

8. What is the main idea of this selection? _____

    _____

Discussing the Reading

Talk about your answers to the following questions.

1. The kind of program in which people such as Alicia and Max appear is called a "soap opera." Do you watch soap operas on TV? If so, which ones do you watch?
2. Tell the plot (story) of your favorite show.
3. What do you think about TV commercials? How are they good? How are they bad? How do they affect you?
4. What are your favorite commercials? Which commercials do you dislike? Why?

PART THREE

BUILDING VOCABULARY;
STUDY SKILLS

The suffix (word ending) often indicates the part of speech of a word. Like the prefix (word beginning), the suffix can also give clues to the meaning of the word. The stem (the main part of the word) has a meaning too.

If you know the meanings of the word parts, you might be able to figure out the meaning of a new word. Here are the meanings of some prefixes, stems, and suffixes.

Prefixes	Meaning	Suffixes	Meaning
dis-	opposite; not	-ology	the study of; the science of
un-	not		
re-	again	-er ⎫	
micro-	small	-ist ⎭	a person who
trans-	across	-scope	an instrument
tele-	far		(something) for seeing

Stems	Meaning
bio	life
astro	star
port	carry; move

Sometimes you will see a word that you already know with a prefix or suffix. *Examples:*

uncrowded

1. not   2. crowded

A definition of *uncrowded* is "not crowded."

nutritionist

2. nutrition   1. a person who

A definition of *nutritionist* is "a person who works in the field of nutrition."

A. Draw lines to divide each word into parts. Then write the meanings of the parts and the definition of each word.

dissimilar

1. _____   2. _____

A definition of *dissimilar* is _____ .

reintroduce

2. _____   1. _____

A definition of *reintroduce* is _____ .

B. Write the meanings of the parts of the following words. Then write the definition of each word.

astrologer

3. _____   2. _____   1. _____

Definition: _____

microbiologist

3. _____   4. _____   2. _____   1. _____

Definition: _____

C. Without a dictionary, match the words with their meanings. Write the correct letters on the lines.

1. __*c*__ transatlantic
2. _____ epidemiologist
3. _____ unlimited
4. _____ microscope
5. _____ transport
6. _____ unintelligent
7. _____ epidemiology
8. _____ telescope
9. _____ microphotograph

a. not intelligent
b. something to help us see things far away
c. across the Atlantic Ocean
d. the study of epidemics
e. a small picture
f. not limited
g. to move something from one place to another
h. a person who studies epidemics
i. something to help us see small things

Study Skill: Using a Dictionary
(Dictionary Definitions)

Some words have only one meaning. You can find the meaning in a dictionary entry, which sometimes includes an example.

A. Read the following two dictionary entries and answer the questions about them.

microscope (5) [may′kr əskowp′], *n.*   an instrument with a piece of special glass, or a combination of pieces of glass, that causes very small things to appear larger so that they become visible for study.

telescope (4) [tel′ əskowp′], *n.*   an instrument for making distant objects seem closer and larger through the use of pieces of curved glass and mirrors. **Ex.** *He was studying the stars through a telescope.*

1.   What part of speech is each word? _____

2.   What is the dictionary definition of *microscope?* _____

_____

3.   What is the definition of *telescope?* _____

_____

4.   In a sentence, give an example of the use of the word *telescope.* _____

_____

Most words, however, have more than one meaning. Often the same word can be more than one part of speech; each part of speech can have a different meaning. *Note:* Usually the various definitions of a word come in a certain order in a dictionary entry: The most common meaning comes first, the least common, last.

Examples: [The word *opposite* is most commonly an adjective (adj.); it can also be a noun (n.) or a preposition (prep.). As an adjective, it has two meanings (numbered 1. and 2. in this dictionary entry).]

opposite (2) [ap′əzit], *adj.*   1. against; exactly at the other extreme; different; contrary. **Ex.** *They held opposite ideas on the subject.*   2. facing each other; on the other side; on the other end. **Ex.** *The two houses are on opposite sides of the street.*   —*n.* that which is opposite or very different. **Ex.** *Happy people and sad people are opposites.*   —*prep.* facing. **Ex.** *We sat opposite each other across the table.*

B. Read the above example. On the lines write answers to the following questions.

1. What part of speech is the word *opposite* when it means "facing"? _____

    Give an example of this use of the word in a sentence: _____

2. This entry gives four explanations of the first adjective meaning of *opposite*.

    What are they? _____

    _____

3. How many explanations does the entry give for the second adjective meaning of

    the word? _____ For its noun meaning? _____

PART FOUR

SCANNING FOR INFORMATION

There is a TV program guide in most newspapers, and you can also buy a TV magazine at the store. Look at the following page from a Houston magazine and then read the questions. Find the information as fast as you can. Write the answers on the lines.

Following are several abbreviations and words from program guides.

❷ = the channel number of a local station

KPRC = the local broadcast station

CBS ⎫
ABC ⎬ national commercial TV networks
NBC ⎭

Ind. = independent TV station

PBS = public broadcasting station (no commercials)

cable TV = services that cost extra money

1. How many "broadcast stations" are there in the Houston area? _____
    Are any of these stations publicly owned (that is, do not depend on money from

    commercials)? _____ If so, how many? _____

2. What is the national network of channel KTRK? _____

3. How many cable TV stations are available in Houston? _____

    Which service offers programs in the Spanish language? _____

    Which offers rock music twenty-four hours a day? _____

    What can you see on "Home Box Office," "Cinemax," and "The Movie

    Channel"?_____

    _____

Channels Listed in Houston Edition

(Programs designated by (BW) are not in color.)

──────── Broadcast Stations ────────

2 KPRC (NBC) **11** KHOU (CBS) **26** KRIV (Ind.)
8 KUHT (PBS) **13** KTRK (ABC) **39** KHTV (Ind.)
20 KTXH (Ind.)

In addition to the listings herein, Ch. 8 schedules instructional programming throughout the broadcast day.

──────── Cable/Pay-TV ────────

(ART) Arts & Entertainment Network
(BET) Black Entertainment Television
(CBN) CBN Cable Network
(CNN) Cable News Network
(ESN) ESPN

(HBO) Home Box Office
(LIF) Lifetime
(MAX) Cinemax
(MTV) Music Television
(NIK) Nickelodeon
(NSH) Nashville Network

(SHO) Showtime
(SIN) Spanish International Network
(TBS) WTBS (Atlanta; Ind.)
(TMC) The Movie Channel
(USA) USA Network
(WGN) WGN (Chicago; Ind.)

C-SPAN provides 24-hour public affairs programs, consisting primarily of coverage of the U.S. House of Representatives. **Music Television** (MTV) is a 24-hour rock-music channel; check listings for details of late-night concerts, movies and interviews presented on weekends.

Symbols for hearing-impaired viewers

(CC) Closed-captioned (Special decoder needed)
(OC) Open-captioned (Visible without decoder)
(S) Interpreted in sign language (Interpreter appears on screen)

Houston Edition

Monday

───── EVENING ─────

6 PM **2** **11** **13** NEWS
8 MacNEIL, LEHRER NEWSHOUR
20 LOVE BOAT—Comedy
The Captain (Gavin MacLeod) tries to lose weight to win an old high-school flame (Jessica Walter); a call girl (Caren Kaye) tries to reform; two singles (Michael Callan, Annette Funicello) whose partners have died vow never to fall in love again. (60 min.)
26 JEFFERSONS (CC)—Comedy
To keep the Help Center afloat, Louise must petition her patronizing former employer (Amzie Strickland) for funds.
39 ONE DAY AT A TIME—Comedy
In a play for attention, Barbara (Valerie Bertinelli) runs off to Chicago for a night with a young man (John Putch).
(CBN) HERE COME THE BRIDES —Comedy-Drama
(CNN) MONEYLINE—Lou Dobbs
(ESN) SPORTSCENTER
(LIF) MOTHER'S DAY—Magazine
(NIK) YOU CAN'T DO THAT ON TELEVISION—Children
(NSH) DANCIN' U.S.A.
(SIN) MALEFICIO—Novela
(USA) RADIO 1990
(WGN) BARNEY MILLER—Comedy
6:05 (TBS) HOGAN'S HEROES—Comedy
6:30 **2** FAMILY FEUD—Game
11 ENTERTAINMENT TONIGHT
Scheduled: David Hasselhoff ("Knight Rider"), Ron Hendren, Mary Hart.

26 THREE'S COMPANY—Comedy
It seems it only takes a fake mustache to make Jack irresistible to Terri.
39 PM MAGAZINE
A woman who survived a crash on her first solo flight; and the Caribbean's Cayman Islands.
(CNN) CROSSFIRE
(ESN) 1982 AFC AND NFC CHAMPIONSHIPS
(HBO) FRAGGLE ROCK—Children
(LIF) '80s WOMAN—Discussion
(NIK) THIRD EYE—Science Fiction
(NSH) YOU CAN BE A STAR
(SIN) VERONICA, EL ROSTRO DEL AMOR—Novela
(USA) DRAGNET—Crime Drama
Friday and Gannon try to find two men who are swindling elderly citizens. Friday: Jack Webb.
(WGN) JEFFERSONS (CC)—Comedy
6:35 (TBS) SANFORD AND SON—Comedy
7 PM **2** TV'S BLOOPERS & PRACTICAL JOKES
Scheduled: Practical jokes on Scott Baio by Mindy Cohn, and David Steinberg by Audrey Landers; New York late-night spots; news and weather bloopers; a "Sports Hall of Shame" segment; sexy foreign commercials; "classic" U.S. commercials. (60 min.)
8 NIGHTLY BUSINESS REPORT
11 SCARECROW AND MRS. KING
Hoping to arrange a spy trade, enemy agents kidnap Amanda (Kate Jackson), but the Agency refuses to trade. Scarecrow: Bruce Boxleitner. Francine: Martha Smith. (Repeat; 60 min.)

4. How many channels offer news at 6:00? _____

5. What channel shows "One Day at a Time" at 6:00? _____

    What kind of program is it? _____

    How do you know? _____

6. What kind of program is "Dragnet" at 6:30? _____

    Who is the main actor in the show? _____

    What part does he play? _____

    What happens in the show on this evening? _____

    Do you need cable TV to watch this show? _____

7. You have children who want to watch TV at 6:30. Which shows might you turn

    on for them? _____

8. Which show or shows might you watch? _____

    Why? _____

Going Beyond the Text

Bring some TV and radio schedules from local newspapers or magazines to class. List
the abbreviations and symbols. Find out their meanings.

Read some of the items aloud. Discuss them. Choose programs to watch or listen to.
After you see or hear the programs, summarize them for the class.

PART FIVE

PERSONAL STORIES

Follow these steps for the stories:

1. Read them quickly and tell the main ideas.
2. Answer your instructor's questions about the stories, or ask and answer questions of your own.
3. Tell your own opinions of the ideas in the stories.
4. Tell or write about your own opinions of television.

Television: Three Views

A   My television is an important piece of furniture to me. I can't get out of the house very often, but my TV brings the whole world to me. From the evening news I learn about reality in the outside world: politics, the environment, recent changes in technology and medicine, and so on. I like game shows and travel programs, too. And I love comedies; I think it's important to be able to laugh.

B   Our son, Bobby, used to spend *hours* each day in front of the "boob tube." He was beginning to get strange ideas of reality from the violence and sex on many programs. Another problem was the commercials for children's toys. Bobby wanted everything he saw. Finally, we decided to have *no* TV. We put the TV set in the garage. Bobby was unhappy about this for a few weeks, but now he's learning more creative ways to spend his time: with friends, toys, books, and us!

C   When I came to this country, I didn't speak any English. I took classes and studied, but it wasn't enough. I wanted to learn faster. I began to watch TV for two hours every day: a half-hour of news, a half-hour comedy program, and a one-hour interview show where people asked and answered a lot of questions. I didn't understand anything at first. But my listening comprehension slowly got better. Now I think of TV as one of my best "teachers."

9

FRIENDS AND SOCIAL LIFE

MEETING THE PERFECT MATE

Getting Started

Look at the picture story and talk about it.

1. Who are the people?
2. What are they talking about? How are the three people different from one another?
3. Do you agree with any one of them? Why or why not?
4. How do young people in your country often meet their future boyfriends/ girlfriends?

126

Preparing to Read

Think about the answers to these questions. (The reading selection will answer them.)

1. What was a common kind of marriage in Korea in the past?
2. How do some Canadians and Americans meet the people who become their boyfriends or girlfriends?
3. What is an advantage to each method (way) to meet people? What is a disadvantage?

Glancing at Vocabulary (optional)

Here are some vocabulary items from the reading selection. You can learn them now or come back to them later.

Nouns	Adjectives	Expressions
date	aggressive	dating
roommate	awful	service
guy	great	arranged
wedding	wonderful	marriage

Verb

match

Read the following selection. Then answer the questions after the reading.

Meeting the Perfect Mate

A   For the past month I've been taking a graduate seminar called "Social Structure." It's a very popular course. We've been discussing friendship, marriage, and other relationships. One of our assignments is to examine the ways that people meet potential husbands and wives. I've been interviewing students on campus all week as part of my study.

First, I talked with my roommate in the dormitory, Sook In, a student from Korea.

"What's one way to meet a possible mate?" I asked her.

"Well," she said, "one method in my country is to have a matched marriage."

"A what?" I asked. "I know you can match a tie to a shirt—or two socks after you do the laundry. But people?"

"Sure," she replied. "There aren't many arranged marriages these days, but there were a lot not too long ago. My parents, for example, met each other for the first time on their wedding day. My grandparents chose their children's mates and arranged the wedding."

"Do you mean that they weren't in love? That sounds awful! Weren't they upset?"

"Maybe a little bit," Sook In said, "but they accepted each other. Then, fortunately, they grew to love each other. They've had a good, successful marriage for the past thirty years. This happens in a lot of arranged marriages."

I shook my head. "Amazing!" I said.

B   The next person that I interviewed was Bill, a guy in my business management class.

"I meet a lot of women in dancing places—at least more than I do on campus," he said. "The environment is interesting and I go every weekend, if possible, to dance or talk or just listen to music."

"That seems great," I said.

"I thought so, too, at first," he said a little sadly. "But on the other hand, very often the women in those places are unfriendly. A lot of men are too aggressive, and the women as a result are very cold."

C   "Dancing places? Never!" said Julie, a student who works part-time in the campus bookstore. "I prefer to make new friends at places where people have interests in common. I met my boyfriend at the health club, for example, and it seems that the healthy atmosphere of the gym is continuing into the relationship that I have with him."

"That sounds wonderful," I said.

"Yes," she said, "I guess so. But to be honest, there's one problem with this arrangement."

"What?" I asked.

"The truth is that I really hate to exercise, so I don't want to go to the gym anymore. What's my boyfriend going to think when he finds this out?"

To be continued . . .

Getting the Main Ideas

Write T (true) or F (false) on the lines.

1. _____   The writer of the selection has been interviewing students about ways to meet people socially.

2. _____   Arranged marriages were always unpopular in Korea because they were usually unpleasant.

3. _____   A dancing place with music is a wonderful place for everyone to meet friendly people.

4. _____   In some places, students can meet people who have common interests.

5. _____   The author of the selection has found a perfect way to meet new friends.

Guessing Meaning from Context

Circle the words in each of the following sentences that give clues to the meaning of the underlined word. Then circle the letter of the word that gives the correct meaning of the underlined vocabulary item.

1. <u>Romance</u> should come naturally. A computer program can't lead to (true love.)

   a. nature   (b.) love   c. technology

2. We've been discussing friendship, marriage, and other <u>relationships</u>.

   a. problems   b. people we like   c. personal connections or associations

3. One of our assignments is to examine the ways that people meet <u>potential</u> husbands and wives. I've been interviewing students on campus. "What's one way to meet a possible <u>mate</u>?" I asked my roommate in the <u>dormitory</u>.

   mate: a. friend   b. marriage   c. husband or wife

   potential: a. matched   b. possible in the future   c. assigned

   dormitory: a. classroom   b. place for interviews   c. place where students live on a campus

4. "Very often the women in dancing places are unfriendly. A lot of men are too aggressive, so the women as a result act very <u>cold</u>."

   a. in need of a sweater   b. sick   c. not friendly

5. "I met my boyfriend at the health club, and it seems that the healthy atmosphere of the <u>gym</u> is continuing into the relationship that I have with him."

   a. dancing place   b. restaurant   c. place to exercise

Recognizing Reading Structure

A. Circle the number of the main idea of the reading.

1. People in dancing places aren't friendly.
2. There are advantages and disadvantages to the various ways to meet people.
3. Health clubs are good places to meet people.
4. Arranged marriages are usually successful.

B. The following outline shows the organization of the topics and ideas in the reading selection. First, on the numbered lines, arrange the following topics in order. Look back at the reading, if necessary.

>   Arranged marriages
>   Meeting people in dancing places
>   Meeting in health clubs
>   Introduction: reason for interviewing people

Then write the following ideas on the correct lettered line under each topic:

>   Mates may meet for the first time on their wedding day.
>   You can talk or just listen to music.
>   Husbands and wives may learn to love each other.
>   The women act unfriendly because a lot of men are too aggressive.
>   People with a common interest in exercise meet here.

1. *Introduction: reasons for interviewing people*

2. _____

   a. *Mates may meet for the first time on their wedding day.*

   b. _____

3. _____

   a. *The dancing and the music are exciting.*

   b. _____

4. _____

   a. _____

Understanding Details

> Often a writer leaves out words because information in other sentences or in another part of the sentence makes them unnecessary.
>
> *Example:*   "What's one way to meet a possible husband or wife?" I asked.
>   "Well," she said, "one method in my country is to have a matched marriage." (Method for what? To find a husband or wife.)

A. In the following sentences there are missing words that we understand. Which words are understood in these sentences? Write them in the blanks.

1. "I know you can match a tie to a shirt—or _you can match_ two socks, too, after you do the laundry. But _can you match_ people?

   "Sure _____ ," she replied. "There aren't many arranged marriages these days, but there were a lot _____ not too many years ago."

2. "Do you mean that they weren't in love? Weren't they upset?"

   "Maybe _____ a little bit _____ ," Sook In said. "But they've had a successful marriage for thirty years."

   I shook my head. "_____ amazing!" I said.

3. "I meet a lot of women in dancing places," Bill said. "The environment of loud music is exciting. I go _____ every weekend, if _____ possible. But a lot of men are too aggressive, and the women as a result _____ very cold."

   "_____ dancing places? _____ never _____ !" said Julie, a student who works in the campus bookstore.

Some words refer to ideas that came before them in the reading.

Example: "My parents have had a good marriage for the past thirty years. This happens in a lot of arranged marriages." (What does *this* refer to? Having a good marriage.)

B. In each of the following sentences, circle the words that the underlined word refers to.

1. I've been taking a (graduate seminar in Social Structure) for the past month. It's a very popular course.

2. "One method is to have a matched marriage," Sook In said. "A what?" I asked.

3. "My grandparents chose their children's mates and arranged the wedding," she explained.

   "Do you mean they weren't in love?"

4. "I meet a lot of women in dancing places—at least more than I <u>do</u> on campus."

5. "Dancing places seem great," I said.

    "I thought <u>so</u> at first, too," he said a little sadly.

6. "It seems that the healthy atmosphere in the gym is continuing into our relationship," she said.

    "<u>That</u> sounds wonderful," I said.

    "Yes," she said, "I guess <u>so</u>."

Now turn back to the "Preparing to Read" section on page 127 and answer the questions.

Discussing the Reading

Talk about your answers to the following questions.

1. Do you know anyone who had an arranged marriage? Are there arranged marriages in your country? What is your opinion of this way to meet potential mates?
2. Have you gone to a health club or exercise class? Did you enjoy it?
3. Where do people with common interests usually meet?

PART TWO

MEETING THE PERFECT MATE (continued)

Glancing at Vocabulary (optional)

Here are some vocabulary items from the next reading selection. You can learn them now or come back to them later.

Nouns	Verbs	Expressions
date	fill (out)	make a mistake
(person)	miss	application form
height		be kidding
feet (')	**Adjectives**	produce section
inches (")	specific	
	general	

Skimming for Main Ideas

Read the following selection quickly.

Meeting the Perfect Mate (continued)

D "Computer dating services are the answer!" said my friend Sara, who lives down the hall from me in the dormitory. "They provide a great way to meet people! The advantage is that you have a lot in common with the people you meet through a computer. The computer can match you up with someone of your same intelligence, astrological sign, age, lifestyle, and personality. For instance, you can meet someone who is creative, competitive, and honest, and you can ask for a scientist, an actor, a vegetarian, or . . ."

"Have you had many successful dates so far?" I asked.

"To tell the truth," she said, "no. I think I made a big mistake when I filled out the application form. I didn't want to miss a wonderful guy because of an answer that was too specific, so I was careful to write very general answers."

"What do you mean?"

"Well, there was a question about height. I said 'anyone between 3'5" and 7'5".' Then there was a question about recreation. I answered 'yes' to forty-seven interests, from gourmet cooking to camping in the wilderness. I wrote that I liked swimming, hiking, the arts, comedy movies, quiz shows, mystery stories, business, ethnic foods, and so on, but I think that the computer got confused. It hasn't found a date for me since I sent in the application."

E Last, I interviewed a guy in the cafeteria.

"Supermarkets," he told me.

"You're kidding," I said.

"No, I'm serious. I meet a lot of potential dates over the frozen pizzas in the convenience-food section. Also, it's easy to make small talk over the tomatoes and lettuce in the produce section. We discuss chemicals and nutrition and food prices. Sometimes this leads to a very romantic date."

I slowly shook my head: it is strange . . . very strange. I bit my lip because I didn't want to be impolite.

That evening, I talked with my roommate, Sook In.

"You know," I said. "I think maybe your parents and grandparents had a pretty good idea. A matched marriage is beginning to seem more and more practical to me."

Inferring: Figuring Out the Meaning

Often a reading selection gives information from which a reader can infer (figure out) other information. Write an X on the line in front of the ideas that the author stated (clearly said) or implied (suggested) in the reading selection. Write an O before the ideas that the writer did not state or imply. Look back at the reading if necessary.

1. __X__   The writer's friend, Sara, is a student.

2. __X__   Sara thinks that computer dating services have many advantages.

3. __O__   There is a computer dating service in the dormitory.

4. _____   A computer application asks questions about height, interests, and other things.

5. _____   The computer tries to match people for dates.

6. _____   Sara wants to have a date with a doctor who doesn't eat meat.

7. _____   She hasn't had much success with computer dating so far.

8. _____   She is a tall woman who likes tall men.

9. _____   She prefers gourmet cooking to camping in the wilderness.

10. _____   The student that the writer interviewed in the cafeteria likes computer dating services, too.

11. _____   He makes small talk with potential dates in stores.

12. _____   He likes to eat pizza with lettuce and tomato salads.

13. _____   He talks about nutrition and natural foods when he goes out on dates.

14. _____   The writer doesn't think that it is a good idea to meet people in the supermarket.

15. _____   The writer didn't tell her opinion to the guy in the cafeteria.

16. _____   She thinks that matched marriages may have some advantages.

Discussing the Reading

Talk about your answers to the following questions.

1. Do you have computer dating services in your country? What do you think of this way to find dates?
2. Do you sometimes make small talk with people in supermarkets? Do these people ever become your friends?
3. Where do you usually meet the people who become your friends? Where do you meet potential boyfriends or girlfriends?

PART THREE

BUILDING VOCABULARY; STUDY SKILLS

A. Without a dictionary, match each word on the left with its meaning. Write the correct letter on the line.

1. _d_ specific
2. ___ cold
3. ___ height
4. ___ miss
5. ___ fill out
6. ___ potential
7. ___ guy
8. ___ produce
9. ___ kidding

a. boy or man
b. not serious
c. write (in a form)
d. the opposite of "general"
e. fruit and vegetables
f. how tall a person or thing is
g. possible
h. unfriendly
i. not find

B. Circle the letters of *all* the words that might fit in each blank.

1. They had a(n) _____ marriage.

   a. great   b. matched   c. romance   d. arranged

2. She went to the _____ to meet people.

   a. application   b. gym   c. café   d. produce section

3. We're going to have a wonderful _____ .

   a. romantic   b. date   c. relationship   d. successful

4. I want a mate who is _____ .

   a. honest   b. successful   c. truth   d. exciting

Sometimes you can tell what part of speech a word is from its suffix. Here are some common suffixes, with their meanings in parentheses.

Nouns	Adjectives
-ship (*condition*)	-ly (*like*)
-ity (*characteristic*)	-ing (*causing a feeling*)
	-ed (*having a feeling*)

Note: An adjective with an *-ed* ending often describes a person.

Example: I get *bored* in cafés. (= Cafés bore me. I have a feeling of boredom when I go to them.)

An adjective with an *-ing* ending can describe a person or a thing.

Examples: Cafés are *boring*. (= Cafés bore me. I feel bored in them.) My date last night was *boring*. (= My date bored me. He wasn't interesting.)

C. In each of the following sections, fill in the blanks with the correct form—noun, verb, adjective, or adverb. Choose from the words above each section. Pay attention to the verb tenses.

relationship	relative	relate	related

1. My mother and my father have a very successful _____ .

2. They always _____ to each other very well.

3. Are you blood _____s or are you _____ by marriage?

person	personality	personal

4. The information on a computer dating form is _____ ; no one else sees it.

5. I met an interesting _____ on a computer date; he had an amazing _____ .

surprise	surprised	surprising	surprised

6. There was a big _____ waiting for me at my dormitory last night.

7. A girlfriend from many years ago _____ me with a visit.

8. I didn't know that she was coming, so I was very _____ .

9. She told me many _____ stories about herself.

friend	friendship	friendly

10. I want to meet people for _____ , not for dates.

11. _____s are more important than potential mates.

12. I like people who are _____ .

Study Skill: Increasing Reading Speed (Matching Synonyms and Opposites)

The following exercises will help you increase your reading speed.

When your teacher tells you to begin each section, look at the underlined word to the left of each line. Read across the line, from left to right, as fast as you can. In the first section, circle the word that has a similar meaning to the underlined word. At the end of each section, write your time (how many seconds it took you to complete the exercises). Try to work faster with each section.

guy	roommate	(man)	mate	match	date
laundry	clothes	dormitory	child care	utilities	stove
wedding	great	wilderness	ethnic	mystery	marriage
cafeteria	channel	adventure	restaurant	movie	nutrition
amazing	aggressive	potential	surprising	arrange	cold

Time: _____

Now circle the word in each line that has approximately the opposite meaning of the underlined word.

<u>exciting</u>	worried	natural	strange	honesty	(boring)
<u>disease</u>	sickness	health	atmosphere	gourmet	romance
<u>accept</u>	confuse	succeed	interview	offer	practical
<u>positive</u>	intelligent	choice	negative	creative	extended
<u>silent</u>	healthy	loud	clear	quiet	real

Time: _____

<u>upset</u>	calm	satisfy	available	dangerous	affect
<u>general</u>	organ	modern	specific	human	specific
<u>personal</u>	indoor	examine	public	computer	clues
<u>solitary</u>	wildlife	protect	common	crowded	expensive
<u>content</u>	share	unhappy	equal	nuclear	situation

Time: _____

Now circle *all* the words that belong in the underlined category.

<u>relatives</u>	(father)	(husband)	(brother)	extended	educated
<u>produce</u>	fruit	chicken	vegetables	strawberries	caviar
<u>weather</u>	outside	wind	vacation	rain	storm
<u>relationship</u>	café	accept	friendship	shirt	marriage
<u>feeling</u>	possible	love	sadness	anger	music

Time: _____

PART FOUR

SCANNING FOR INFORMATION

Many college newspapers and some neighborhood newspapers have a section for news of social events. This section answers the questions "What can I do for fun this weekend?" and "Where can I meet people?"

Look at the newspaper section on the next page and then read the questions. Find the information as fast as you can and write the answers on the lines.

1.
TRAVELOG FILMS "Valley of Light" (Yosemite), "Simpatico Means Venezuela," "People of the Amazon" and "Assignment Yellowbird" (Florida and the Bahamas) are presented Saturday, October 15, 2:30 p.m. at the Santa Monica Public Library, 1343 Sixth St., Santa Monica. 451-5751.

2.
WANTED: FRIENDLY people to join me on all day sailing excursions, weekdays and weekends. No experience required, will teach. Leave message at 473-8550.

3.
POET ROBERT Mezey reads from his works Wednesday, October 19, 4-6 p.m. in CalArts Langley Hall. 805-255-1050.

4.
WEST VALLEY Jewish Singles, ages 18-28, attend Friday Night Services Friday, October 14, 8 p.m. at Temple Aliyah. Socializing and desert afterwards at a nearby coffee shop. Call Gregg, 703-0033, for details.

5.
SINGLE PARENTING—A one-day workshop for divorced single parents experiencing difficulties balancing the delicate and difficult act of being single and being a parent. Saturday, October 29, 9:30 a.m. to 4 p.m. at AID-WEST. Call Dr. Wilma Awerbuch at 824-0211 to register./   t l

6.
"WALKIN' SINGLES" takes semi-strenuous stroll through Marina del Rey Saturday, October 15, 1:30 p.m. meeting at 4754 Admiralty Way (in Boys Market parking lot). Historical narration. Age range 29-45 only. No smoking. Potluck picnic follows. To be included, phone 789-1035.   t52

7.
DR. ALAN H. Pressman discusses "Designing Your Diet" Friday, October 14, 7 p.m. at 845 N. Highland Ave. 871-2222.

8.
ROOKERY READINGS present poets Lance Jencks and Gerald Locklin, folksinger Michael Gleason and artist Debra Williams Tuesday, October 18, 8:30 p.m. at the Upstart Crow and Company, South Coast Village, Santa Ana. $2. 714-826-3094.

9.
"STARTING AND Managing Your Own Business" is offered Friday, October 14, 1-6 p.m. at USC. 743-2098.

10.
SAVE THE ANIMALS Fund is presenting The Animal Film, a comprehensive survey of the injustices committed against animals in the western society. Free showing Saturday, October 15, 12:30 p.m. at The Orange Room Cafeteria, Dept. of Water and Power, 111 N. Hope St. opposite the Music Center. Free parking Gate 6. 484-8766./

11.
BACH TO BLUES trio. Free concert Wednesday, October 19, 2 p.m. at Fairfax Library, †61 S. Gardner near Third.

12.
GAVIN DILLARD reads from his book "Notes From a Marriage: Love Poems" Sunday, October 16, 3 p.m. at A Different Light Bookstore, 4014 Santa Monica Blvd. 668-0629.

13.
"COPING WITH Stress: Basic Relaxation Methods" is discussed Wednesday, October 19, 7-8:30 p.m. at the Hollywood Presbyterian Medical Center, 1300 N. Vermont Ave. 660-3530, ext. 6350.

1. Match the social events in the newspaper section to the following interests. Write the numbers of the events on the lines.

   _____   animal life   _____   a healthy diet

   _____   travel around the world   _____   social life for single Jewish
                                                           people
   _____   classical and jazz music
                                                 _____   poetry
   _____   being a better single
            (unmarried or divorced) parent   _____   sailing (traveling on a boat)

   _____   business   _____   walking for health

   _____   learning ways to relax

2. Where might you meet people who share your interest in animals? _____

   _____

   What will you do in this place? _____

   How much do tickets cost to this event? _____

3. If you want to meet single people—and you like exercise and history—what

   phone number can you call for information? _____

   How old will the people at this event be? _____

   Can you smoke at this event? _____

4. When can you hear a concert of classical and jazz music? _____

   _____

5. Which event or events from page 140 interest you? Why? _____

   _____

Going Beyond the Text

Bring to class the "calendar" section of your newspaper or other articles with information about things to do and places to go in your city. List the new vocabulary items and find out their meanings. Read several items aloud and explain them to the class. Discuss the events and places. Choose one or more places to visit or events to attend. Make arrangements with one or more classmates to go there. Then describe your experience to the class.

PART FIVE

PERSONAL STORIES

Follow these steps for the stories:

1. Read them quickly and tell the main ideas.
2. Answer your instructor's questions about the stories, or ask and answer questions of your own.
3. Tell your own opinions of the ideas in the stories.
4. Tell or write about your own opinions of social life in this country.

Social Life in the United States: Two Views

A   I think I made a big mistake when I decided to come to this country. The educational system is okay, and in general it's a comfortable place to live, but life here can be very lonely. It's difficult to have close relationships with people here. Some Americans seem to hate foreigners. They're very cold to anyone different from them. Others are friendly at first, but they aren't really interested in a close friendship with a new person. And dating is impossible! I've dated several American women since I came here, but this hasn't been very successful. American women are too independent, too aggressive. Sometimes *they* suggest a place to go on a date. Sometimes they even want to pay for the dinner or movie. They don't understand romance.

B   Some of the other students in my ESL class aren't very happy here in the United States because they don't have friends. I know it isn't easy, but they should try harder. I've been living here for a year and a half, and I've learned a lot about relationships with Americans. First, Americans who are interested in other cultures are friendly to foreign students. It's a good idea to spend time with such people; try folk dance clubs, international student groups, and so on. Second, it's important to be positive; don't tell a new American friend, "Your government is terrible. Americans are impolite. Your customs are wrong." Third, be open to new ideas. Customs aren't "right" or "wrong"—just different.

10

CUSTOMS, CELEBRATIONS, AND HOLIDAYS

PART ONE

SOCIAL CUSTOMS: A DINNER PARTY

Getting Started

Look at the picture and talk about it.

1. Where is the young man? What is he doing?
2. Why does he look confused? What is his problem?
3. What do you think he should do in this situation?
4. Have you ever had a problem like this? What did you do about it?

Preparing to Read

Think about the answers to these questions. (The reading selection will answer them.)

1. Who wrote the letters in the reading? Who answered them?
2. Should you bring something when you go to someone's house for dinner? If so, what?
3. At what time should you arrive for a dinner party?
4. What can you do if you don't know which knife, fork, or spoon to use at a formal dinner party?
5. If you give a dinner party, how can you help your guests feel comfortable?
6. What are some secrets of a successful dinner party?

Glancing at Vocabulary (optional)

Here are some vocabulary items from the reading selection. You can learn them now or come back to them later.

Nouns	Verbs	Adjectives	Expressions
invitation	arrive	late	make a mistake
kindness	thank	early	let someone know
card	finish	(un)comfortable	thank-you note
	act		spend time

Read the following selection quickly. Then answer the questions after the reading.

Social Customs: A Dinner Party

A   Dear Etty Kit,

My roommate's family wants me to celebrate Thanksgiving with them in their home. I accepted the invitation, and I'm excited about going, but I'm a little nervous about it, too. The social customs in my country are very different from here, so I'm a little worried about making mistakes.

Should I bring a gift, such as candy or flowers? Should I arrive on time or a little late? At the dinner table, how can I know which fork or knife to use? How can I let the family know that I'm thankful for their kindness?

Confused

B   Dear Confused,

It's a good idea to bring a small gift when you go to a dinner party. Flowers are always nice, or you might bring a bottle of wine if you know that the family drinks it.

You should arrive on time or five to ten minutes late. Don't get there early. If you're going to be more than fifteen minutes late, you should call and tell them.

Try to relax at the dinner table. If you're confused about choosing the correct fork, knife, or spoon, just watch the other guests, and follow them. If you still have no idea of what to do, don't be shy about asking the person next to you; it's better to ask than to be silently uncomfortable and nervous.

If you like the food, say so. Of course, you'll thank the host and hostess for the meal and for their kindness. It's also a good idea to send a card or thank-you note the day after.

Etty Kit

C   Dear Ms. Kit,

I'm going to give a dinner party next month for some Canadian friends. I want my guests to enjoy themselves and to feel comfortable. What's the secret of giving a successful party?

Worried

D   Dear Worried,

Cook something that lets you spend time with your guests. If a guest offers to help you in the kitchen, accept the offer. It often makes people feel more comfortable when they can help.

Before serving dinner, while your guests make small talk in the living room, offer them drinks. Those who drink alcohol might like liquor or wine, but make sure to provide soft drinks and fruit juice for people who don't. At the dinner table, let your guests serve themselves. Offer them a second serving after they finish, but don't ask more than once or twice. Most guests will take more if they want it.

Perhaps the most important rule of all is to be natural. Treat your guests as you want them to treat you when you're in their home—that is, act naturally toward them, and don't try *too* hard to be polite. Have a good time in a pleasant atmosphere.

Etty Kit

Getting the Main Ideas

Write T (true), F (false), or I (impossible to know from the reading) on the lines.

1. _____   People write letters to Etty Kit and she gives advice about social rules and customs.

2. _____   There are no social rules for dinner parties in the United States and Canada.

3. _____   It's very important to leave a party on time.

4. _____   When you give a party, you should spend all your time in the kitchen.

5. _____   You should always make enough food for your guests to have two or three servings.

6. _____   For both the guests and the hosts, it's important to feel comfortable and not try too hard to be polite.

7. _____   Americans and Canadians have a lot of dinner parties.

Guessing Meaning from Context

Circle the words in each of the following sentences that give clues to the meaning of the underlined words. Then circle the letter of the answer.

1. My roommate's family wants me to celebrate Thanksgiving with them in their home on November 23. I accepted the dinner invitation, but I'm feeling a little nervous about it.

   a. a special day for a dinner party
   b. a thank-you note
   c. a celebration for roommates

2. Should I bring a gift such as candy or flowers?

   a. something to eat
   b. something to give another person
   c. plants

3. You should arrive on time or five to ten minutes late. Don't get there early.

   on time: a. early   b. not late   c. at 8:00
   get there: a. come to a place b. have something c. eat dinner

4. Don't be shy about asking; it's better to ask than to feel uncomfortable and nervous.

   a. comfortable   b. loud   c. not comfortable

5. After a dinner party, of course, you'll thank the host and hostess for the meal and for their kindness.

   host and hostess: a. guests   b. people who give a party   c. cooks
   meal: a. party   b. gift   c. dinner

6. Be sure to provide soft drinks and fruit juice for people who don't drink alcohol.

   a. juice   b. fruit drinks   c. drinks without alcohol

7. At the dinner table, let your guests serve themselves. Offer them a second serving after they finish.

   serve: a. give food to   b. talk to   c. begin eating
   serving: a. dessert   b. conversation   c. amount of food

Recognizing Reading Structure

A. Circle the number of the main idea of the reading.

1. Always bring a nice gift when you go to a dinner party.
2. Just watch the guests at a party and follow them, and do not be shy about asking questions.
3. There are no secrets to giving a successful party.
4. If you follow a few simple rules for dinner parties, you can have a good time in a pleasant atmosphere.

B. Following is the organization of topics in the reading selection. Write in the missing words; choose from the words *guest* or *host*.

1. Letter from a ___*guest*___ who is going to a dinner party.

2. Answer to the _____

3. Letter from a _____ who is going to give a party.

4. Answer to the _____

C. The following ideas are from the reading. On the line next to each idea, write the letter of the section that the idea is from.

1. __*B*__   It's a good idea to bring the host or hostess a gift.

2. _____   You should arrive at a party on time or a few minutes late.

3. _____   I'm nervous about going to a dinner party.

4. _____   I want my guests to enjoy themselves at a party that I'm going to give.

5. _____   Spend as much time with your guests as possible.

6. _____   When should I arrive at a dinner party?

7. _____   How do I choose the correct knife, fork, or spoon?

8. _____   Offer your guests drinks before dinner.

9. _____   How should I thank my host and hostess?

10. _____   Let your guests serve themselves at dinner.

11. _____   Watch the other guests at the table to find out what to do.

12. _____   Thank the host and hostess after the party and the next day.

Understanding Details

In the blanks of the following sentences, write the words that are understood.

1. My roommate's family wants me to celebrate Thanksgiving with them in their home. I accepted the invitation, and I'm excited about going *to their home* .

2. The social customs in my country are very different from _____ here.

3. If you still have no idea what to do at the dinner table, don't be shy about asking the person next to you _____ .

4. Of course, you'll thank the host and hostess for the meal. It's also a good idea to send a card or thank-you note the day after _____ .

5. Those who drink alcohol might like liquor or wine, but be sure to provide soft drinks and fruit juice for those who don't _____ .

6. Offer them a second serving after they finish _____ , but don't ask _____ more than once or twice. Most guests will take more _____ if they want it.

7. Perhaps the most important rule of all _____ is to act natural.

In each of the following sentences, circle the words that the underlined word refers to.

8. I'm excited about going, but I'm a little nervous about <u>it</u>, too.

9. You might bring a bottle of wine if you know that the family drinks <u>it</u>. If you're going to be more than fifteen minutes late, you should call and tell <u>them</u>.

10. If you like the food, say <u>so</u>.

Now turn back to the "Preparing to Read" section on page 145 and answer the questions.

Discussing the Reading

Talk about your answers to the following questions.

1. In your country, is it a good idea to arrive early, on time, or late for a dinner party? How late is "too late"?
2. Is it the custom in your country to bring a gift to the host or hostess? If so, what kind of gift?
3. Have you ever been to a dinner in a Canadian or American home? How was it similar to dinner parties in your country? How was it different?
4. Look at the picture at the beginning of the chapter. How is the table setting different from one in your country? What do you think each fork, knife, and spoon is used for?
5. In your country, do guests serve themselves, or does the host or hostess serve them? What is polite to do at a formal dinner party? What is not polite?

PART TWO

A TRADITIONAL HOLIDAY

Glancing at Vocabulary (optional)

Here are some vocabulary items from the next reading selection. You can learn them now or come back to them later.

Nouns	Verbs	Expressions
symbol	hold	birth of Christ
ghost	rule	"Trick or treat!"
witch	frighten	Lord of the Dead
history		dress up
origin	**Adjectives**	ring doorbells
spirit	uneducated	
magic	religious	
festival	holy	
harvest		
broomstick	**Adverb**	
god	unusually	
goddess		
costume		

Skimming for Main Ideas

The title of a paragraph should indicate the main topic.

A. Read the following four paragraphs quickly. Then put each of the following titles on the correct line.

Witches: A Symbol of Halloween	The First Halloween
Halloween Today	The Origin of Halloween Customs

A Traditional Holiday

[A] *The First Halloween*
_____

Hundreds of years before the birth of Christ, the Celts—the inhabitants of France and the British Isles—held a festival at the beginning of every winter for the Lord of the Dead. These people believed that this god ruled the world in winter, when he called together the ghosts of dead people. On October 31, these spirits of the dead came back in the forms of animals, with very bad ghosts as black cats. At their festival on this day, the Celts used to make big fires to frighten the ghosts and chase them away. This celebration was the beginning of the holiday of Halloween.

[B] _____

The Romans, who ruled the British Isles after the birth of Christ, also held a celebration at the beginning of winter. Because winter was harvest time, the Romans brought apples and nuts for the goddess of gardens. Later, the Christians added their customs to those of the Celts and the Romans. They had a religious holiday on November 1 for the saints (the unusually good people in Christianity), which they called All Hallows' or All Saints' Day. The evening before this day was All Hallows' Even ("holy evening"); later the name became Halloween.

[C] _____

Long ago in Britain, people used to go to wise old women called "witches" to learn about the future. They believed that these witches had the power to tell the future and to use magic words to protect people or change them. There were many beliefs about witches, who are now a symbol of Halloween. For example, people believed witches flew on broomsticks to big, secret meetings, where they ate, sang, and danced. The Christians tried to stop people from believing in witches, but many uneducated people, especially in the countryside, held on to their beliefs.

[D] _____

When people came to North America from the British Isles, they brought their Halloween customs with them. Today, Halloween is a night when children dress up like ghosts, witches, devils, and so on. They go from house to house in their costumes, ring doorbells, and shout, "Trick or treat!" People give them candy, apples, gum, and nuts, and the children have a good time. But most children have no idea that their holiday has such a long history.

You can find out the main idea of a paragraph if you ask the questions "who," "what," "when," "where," "how," or "why" about the topic. By putting together the answers to these questions, you will get the main idea.

Example: paragraph A) Who celebrated? *the Celts*   What? *a festival*
Why? *for the Lord of the Dead* When? *at the beginning of winter*
The main idea of this paragraph is that *the Celtic festival at the beginning of winter for the Lord of the Dead was the first Halloween*

B. Answer the following questions about paragraphs B, C, and D. Then put together the answers to complete the main ideas.

PARAGRAPH B

1.   Who celebrated the harvest? _____

2.   Who celebrated All Saints' Day? _____

3.   The main idea: The customs of _____

_____.

PARAGRAPH C

1.   What did people long ago in Britain believe in? _____

2.   Why? _____

3.   The main idea: _____ ,

a symbol of Halloween.

PARAGRAPH D

1.   Who celebrates Halloween now? _____

2.   Why? _____

3.   The main idea: Halloween today _____

_____

_____.

Now reread the four paragraphs on pages 152 to 153. Try to guess the meaning of the new words from the context. Use your dictionary only when absolutely necessary. Then complete the following exercise.

Inferring: Figuring Out the Meaning

Write an X on the lines in front of the ideas that the author stated (clearly said) or implied (suggested) in the reading selection. Write an O before the ideas that the writer did not say or imply (even if the ideas are true). Look back at the reading if necessary.

1. __X__   Halloween began a long time before the birth of Christ.

2. __X__   Ideas about ghosts, black cats, and witches are part of the celebration of Halloween.

3. __O__   People today put fire in pumpkins (jack-o'-lanterns) to scare away ghosts.

4. _____   The Romans were Christians.

5. _____   People associate apples and nuts with Halloween because they were symbols of the harvest in Roman times.

6. _____   One of the origins of Halloween was religious.

7. _____   The belief in witches came from Christianity.

8. _____   Witches could really fly and had the power of magic.

9. _____   Halloween customs came to the United States from Britain.

10. _____   The custom of trick-or-treating in costumes comes from the days of the Celts.

11. _____   If people do not give treats to children on Halloween, they might play tricks; thus, Halloween is a very dangerous holiday.

12. _____   People in many countries celebrate Halloween today.

Discussing the Reading

Talk about your answers to the following questions.

1. Have you ever celebrated Halloween? If so, how did you celebrate it?
2. What two colors have you noticed at Halloween time? Can you guess what they mean?
3. Do you celebrate Halloween or a similar holiday in your culture?
4. Do some people in your culture believe in witches or in other people who tell the future?

PART THREE

BUILDING VOCABULARY; STUDY SKILLS

In each of the following sections, fill in the blanks with the correct word form—noun, verb, adjective, or adverb. Choose from the words at the beginning of each section. Pay attention to verb tenses and add "-s" to plural nouns.

1. festival   festive

    The Celts had a _____ for the Lord of the Dead. It was a _____ celebration.

2. ruler   rule   spirit   spiritual

    These people had a _____ belief that the god of death _____ the world in winter. He was the _____ of the _____ of dead people.

3. fright   frighten   frightening

    That witch costume looks terrible; it is very _____ . The child in the ghost costume tried to _____ me. She gave me a _____ .

4. god   goddess   harvest   harvested

    The Celts celebrated the festival of Samhain; he was the _____ of the dead. When the Romans _____ their food, they gave thanks to Pomona; she was the _____ of gardens and the _____ .

5. religion   religious   Christ   Christian   Christianity

    The _____ of _____ began with Jesus. No one was _____ before the birth of _____ . _____ people believed in some kind of god.

6. magic   magical   education   educated   uneducated

    In Britain, _____ people used to believe in the _____ of witches. _____ people, however, did not believe that witches had _____ powers. _____ changed their beliefs.

7. symbol   symbolic   custom   customary   costume

The colors orange and black are two _____ of Halloween today.

Orange is _____ of the harvest; black, of death. Putting candles in

pumpkins with faces is a _____ of Halloween. It is _____ to

place these jack o' lanterns in the window for children in _____ who

are going trick or treating.

8. invitation   invite   dress   dress   dressy

If someone _____ you to a party, he or she may send a written

_____ . At a _____ party, men usually wear suits, and

women, _____ . At a Halloween party, people usually

_____ in costumes.

Study Skill: Using a Dictionary
(Words with More Than One Meaning)

> Most common words have more than one meaning. Often the same word can be
> more than one part of speech; each part of speech can have different meanings.

A. Read the following dictionary entries and answer the questions about them.

knife (2) [nayf'],*n.*   a sharp blade for cutting, attached to a handle. —*v.* cut with a knife. **Ex.** *He was knifed in the back by the robber.*

witch (3) [wič], *n.* 1. a woman believed to practice evil magic. **Ex.** *The villagers thought a witch caused their trouble.* 2. an ugly old woman. **Ex.** *The old witch shouted at the children.*

1. How many parts of speech is the word *knife?* _____

The word *witch?* _____

2. Which definition (noun or verb) of *knife* means "an object on the dinner table"?

_____

What is the other definition of the word? _____

3. Which definition (1 or 2) of *witch* is associated with the holiday of Halloween?

_____ Which is the other definition of the word? _____

_____

B. Read the following dictionary entries, paying close attention to the parts of speech, the different meanings, and the examples for each meaning. On the lines, write the part of speech and the number of the appropriate meaning for the underlined word in each sentence.

soft (1) [soft'], *adj.*   1. easily shaped, formed, etc.; yielding to the touch or pressure. **Ex.** *She likes to sleep on a soft bed.*   2. not strong, bright, sharp, etc. **Ex.** *A soft wind was blowing.* 3. gentle; tender; full of sympathy. **Ex.** *He spoke roughly to conceal his soft heart.*   4. smooth; delicate. **Ex.** *The baby's skin was very soft.* 5. quiet. **Ex.** *He spoke in a soft voice.* —**soft'en,** v. make or become soft. —**soft'ly,** *adv.*   —**soft'ness,** n.

shy (4) [šay'], *adj.*   easily frightened; not at ease with others. **Ex.** *She is a shy child.* —*v.* draw back suddenly; start. **Ex.** *The horse shied at the approaching car.*   —**shy'ly** *adv.*   —shy'ness, *n.*

rule (1) [ruwl'], *n.*   1. an order; a guide for conduct which has been established. **Ex.** *Students must obey the school rules.*   2. the usual way of doing things; one's regular practice; usual behavior. **Ex.** *It is their rule to eat dinner late.*   3. the government of a king or other person in authority. **Ex.** *His rule over the country lasted thirty years.*   *v.* 1. govern; control. **Ex.** *The queen ruled her country well.* 2. decide officially. **Ex.** *The court ruled that their activities were punishable*   **rul'er,** *n.* a person who rules a country. **Ex.** *The country has had only three rulers during this century.*   —**as a rule,** generally; most often. **Ex.** *As a rule, he will not go to meetings.*   —**rule out,** eliminate from consideration. **Ex.** *He ruled out going back to school.*

1. The child had hard and <u>soft</u> candy in her Halloween bag.

_____

2. The weather was beautiful; there was a <u>soft</u> breeze blowing.

_____

3. You have to shout "Trick or treat!" Don't say it <u>softly</u>.

_____

4. The child <u>shied</u> away from the frightening witch.

_____

5. I am too <u>shy</u> to wear a funny costume to a party. _____

6. As a <u>rule</u>, children like holidays. _____

7. Our front porch was a kind of social center; there were special <u>rules</u> for making small talk there. _____

8. What god <u>ruled</u> the world in the summer? _____

9. How long did people believe in the <u>rule</u> of the god of death?

_____

PART FOUR

SCANNING FOR INFORMATION

Sometimes we want to send someone a greeting card. It is important to send a card with the correct message (words) inside.

Look at the following cards and answer the questions about them on page 160.

1.

You're Invited

For a New Year's Eve party

Date New Year's Eve

Time 8:00 pm

Place 345 N. Elm Road

R.S.V.P.   B.Y.O.B.

2.

May your birthday be delightful,
Your very best one yet,
A happy, carefree kind of day
That you won't soon forget--
And may the year that follows
Be bright and happy, too,
And bring the very loveliest
And nicest things to you!

*Have a
Wonderful Day*

3.

Just a little note to say
Thank you very much--
When it comes to pleasing people,
You have the perfect touch!

4.

In times of sorrow,
when words of comfort
are needed most, it seems they are
most difficult to say.
May you find comfort
in the thoughts and sympathy
of friends.

5.

As we greet the harvest season
in a joyful, grateful way,
Warm wishes go to your home
for a glad Thanksgiving Day,
And may the year that lies ahead
bring happiness and love
And all the special blessings
that you're so deserving of.

6.

HOPE
HALLOWEEN
TREATS YOU
TO LOTS
OF FUN!

7.

Sorry to hear
of your hospital stay...
Hope you're improving
with every new day,
And before long you'll feel
well and happy again--
You'll be in my thoughts
and my wishes till then.

Hope You're Home Soon

8.

Announcing
name *Breton (Bret) Lee*
arrived *March 27*
weighing *8* lbs *4* oz
parents *Marv + Nancy*

1. Which card is appropriate (correct) to send to someone on Halloween? Write its number: _____

2. Which card is appropriate to send to a new widow? _____

3. Which card might you receive on your birthday? _____

4. Which card should you send to someone who is sick? _____

5. You went to a formal dinner party. You want to send a thank-you note to the hostess. Which do you send? _____

6. Which card might you receive on Thanksgiving? _____

7. A friend of yours recently had a baby. Which card did you receive? _____

8. Which card is an invitation to a party? _____ What time does this party begin? _____ How late (at least) does this party last? _____ What two things should the guests do for this party? _____ How do you know this? _____

9. Where should you send card 7? _____

10. Which card would you like to receive? _____ Why? _____

Going Beyond the Text

Spend some time in the greeting card section of a drugstore or in a card shop at holiday time. Look at the different kinds of cards and other holiday items. Copy some of the messages from cards. Discuss the experience with the class. What kinds of cards did you see? What were their purposes? What items did you see? What do people do with these things?

Read aloud some of the messages that you copied. Discuss new vocabulary. The class tries to guess the occasion (purpose) of the card that the messages came from.

What did you learn about North American holidays and customs from the cards? Discuss your ideas with the class.

PART FIVE

PERSONAL STORIES

Follow these steps for the stories:

1. Read them quickly and tell the main ideas.
2. Answer your instructor's questions about the stories, or ask and answer questions of your own.
3. Tell your own opinions of the ideas in the stories.
4. Tell or write about your own opinions of a holiday in North America or in your culture.

Two Views of Christmas

 Every December, I begin to feel uncomfortable. Why? Christmas is coming. Most people enjoy this holiday, but it makes me depressed. First, I'm not a religious person. This holiday celebrates the birth of Christ, and it's full of religious symbols. Second, Christmas is becoming more and more commercial. It's the most important time of year for owners of stores, for example. Spending lots of money seems to be people's main activity in December. Everywhere  you hear the command, "Buy! Spend! Give!" It's awful. Last, I think Christmas is a difficult time of year for people without families. I've been living away from my family for several years, and I miss being with them —especially at Christmas.

Christmas is my favorite holiday. I love baking Christmas cookies and planning parties. I love sending cards and hearing from old friends. I love seeing children open their gifts on Christmas morning. Most of all, I love one special custom that we have in our family. On the night before Christmas, we dress up in warm clothing and go from house to house in our neighborhood. At each house, we sing Christmas songs. Then we go to a hospital or a home for elderly people and we sing there. We want to let people know that we care about them. Afterward, we come home and drink hot chocolate by the fireplace. I love this!

11

RECREATION

THE OLYMPIC GAMES

Getting Started

Look at the pictures and talk about them.

1. What is the topic of each of the pictures on these pages?
2. What is each person doing?
3. Do you participate in many of these activities?
4. Where do you think people might find these signs?

Preparing to Read

Think about the answers to these questions. (The reading selection will answer them.)

1. When and where were the first Olympic games? Who participated in them?
2. How are the modern Olympics different from the ancient ones?
3. What are some examples of exciting moments in the modern Olympics?
4. How have politics affected the Olympics?
5. What are some problems of the modern Olympics?

Glancing at Vocabulary (optional)

Here are some vocabulary items from the reading selection. You can learn them now or come back to them later.

Nouns		Adjective	Verbs	Expressions
race	spectator	ancient	participate	olive leaves
silver	honor		avoid	a thin line
participation	event	**Connecting Words**	win	take place
century	gold	nevertheless	lose	fourth place
crown	politics	moreover	allow	B.C./A.D.

Read the following selection quickly. Then answer the questions about the reading.

The Olympic Games

A   Although we do not know the exact origins of the earliest Olympic games, we do know that the ancient Greeks had a festival in which athletes competed in sports. This celebration was held regularly every four years and was open to all men and boys who spoke Greek as their native language. These ancient games were simpler than our modern ones. For the month before the festival, the athletes attended a formal course of exercise at the gymnasium in the city of Olympia. Then the competition itself consisted of a single footrace. Later festivals included such sports as jumping, wrestling, discus throwing, and horse racing.

B   These early Olympic games were most popular around the fifth century B.C. (before the birth of Christ). At that time, winning at a sport brought the highest possible honor to the individual competitor, his family, and his city. The winner of a game received neither gold nor silver but a simple crown of olive leaves. Later, however, when the Greeks began paying athletes, there were problems with professionalism. In addition, instead of participating in all sports, the competitors began to specialize; that is, they concentrated on only one Olympic event. Because of this interest in money and the increasing specialization of athletes, the ancient games lost their original purpose; they ended in A.D. 393.

C   The first of the modern Olympics took place in the same country as the original festivals: Two hundred eighty-five athletes from thirteen countries competed in Athens in 1896. Today, thousands of athletes from over one hundred countries compete—each time in a different city of the world. The games are popular, spectacular events. There have been hundreds of exciting, very special Olympic moments that people all over the world have shared by reading newspaper stories, watching films, or seeing the actual events on TV or in person.

D   In 1904, for example, the Cuban runner Felix Carvajal lost his money in New Orleans and could not afford to take the train to St. Louis, Missouri, where the games were taking place. Nevertheless, he participated in the twenty-six-mile Olympic marathon. To do this, he had to run the seven hundred miles to St. Louis. He arrived just in time for the beginning of the marathon. Moreover, after already running seven hundred miles, he succeeded in finishing the marathon in fourth place. Another runner, black American Jesse Owens, won four gold medals and the hearts of the world in the 1936 Olympics in Berlin. As he received his medals, the ruler of Germany, Adolf Hitler, stared coldly from his seat.

E   War between Greek cities stopped the ancient games only twice in one thousand years: Politics rarely entered into the Olympic games. In modern times, however, such has not been the case. Political conflicts have influenced the games more often than just during the rule of Hitler: World war stopped the celebration of the Olympics in 1916, and the same thing happened in 1940 and 1944; because of South African politics, people continue to argue over the participation of athletes from that country; and at the 1972 games in Munich, political terrorists from the Middle East killed seventeen people. Since then many countries have avoided the games for political reasons.

F   In addition to politics, there have been problems with the athletes who compete in the games. Some have used illegal drugs and chemicals. Furthermore, as in the ancient Greek festivals, there have been increasing problems with the professionalism of modern athletes. In general, only "amateurs" are supposed to compete in the Olympics, but the exact line between "amateur" and "professional" can be a thin one. For these reasons, participants and spectators worry about the future of the Olympic games.

Getting the Main Ideas

Write T (true) or F (false), or I (impossible to know from the reading) on the lines.

1. _____ The original Olympic games were held in Greece before the birth of Christ, every four years except in time of war.

2. _____ The old games were more exciting than the modern ones.

3. _____ The first Olympic athletes participated for money and for political reasons.

4. _____ The modern games are so spectacular that no sports event can match them.

5. _____ Politics haven't had an effect on the modern Olympics.

6. _____ The modern Olympics have some of the same problems that the original ones had.

Guessing Meaning from Context

Sometimes the context gives only very general clues to the meaning of a new vocabulary item.

Example: The *athletes* traveled to Greece. (What are athletes? They are probably people because they went somewhere, but what kind of people are they? The context gives no clues.)

Sometimes the context gives more specific clues.

Example: The *athletes* traveled to Greece for the Olympic games. (What kind of people are athletes? They are people who are interested in the Olympics.)

Sometimes the context gives enough clues for the reader to figure out the exact meaning.

Example: The *athletes* traveled to Greece to participate in the sports events of the Olympic games. (What are athletes? They are people who participate in sports events.)

A. Try to figure out the definition of the underlined word in each of the following sentences. Note that each sentence adds a little more information, so that the choices become more and more specific. Circle the letter of the word that gives the correct meaning.

1. Two hundred eighty-five <u>competitors</u> from thirteen countries came.

   a. countries   b. people   c. things

2. Two hundred eighty-five <u>competitors</u> from thirteen countries came to participate.

   a. people who do   b. people who watch   c. things from other
       something   countries

3. Two hundred eighty-five <u>competitors</u> from thirteen countries came to participate in the sports events.

   a. runners   b. watchers   c. athletes

4. The two hundred eighty-five <u>competitors</u> from thirteen countries who came to participate in the sports events all hoped to win.

   a. people who pay   b. people who try to   c. people from differ-
       money   win something   ent countries

B. Try to use the context clues to write more and more specific definitions of the underlined word in each of the following sentences.

1. He participated in the marathon. _____

2. The Cuban runner Felix Carvajal participated in the marathon. _____
    _____

3. The Cuban runner Felix Carvajal participated in the twenty-six mile marathon; he finished the race in fourth place. _____
    _____

*   *   *

4. The competitors began to specialize. _____
    _____

5. Instead of participating in all sports, the competitors began to specialize. _____
    _____

6. Instead of participating in all sports, the competitors began to specialize by concentrating on only one event. _____
    _____

C. Circle the words that give clues to the meaning of the underlined word in each of the following sentences. Then write a definition of each word on the line. Check your answer in a dictionary.

1. Another runner, Jesse Owens, won four events in the 1936 Olympics. As he received his gold medals, Adolf Hitler stared coldly from his seat. _____
    _____

2. Political conflicts have often influenced the games; world war stopped the celebration of the Olympics in 1916, 1940, and 1944. _____

3. At the 1972 games in Munich, political terrorists from the Middle East killed seventeen people. _____

4. Only "amateurs" are allowed to compete in the Olympics, but the line between "amateur" and "professional" can be a thin one.
    _____

Recognizing Reading Structure

A. Circle the number of the main idea of the reading.

1. The modern Olympics are popular, spectacular events that people all over the world enjoy.
2. The ancient Olympics consisted of fewer events than the modern ones.
3. Today, thousands of athletes from over one hundred countries compete in the Olympics.
4. The modern Olympics share some similar special moments but also face some of the same problems as the ancient Olympics.

B. The information in the reading selection can be organized in different ways. Here is an outline of one way; find the outlined topics in the reading and, in the parentheses, write the letters of the paragraphs where the topics appear. (Note that one paragraph may discuss more than one topic and that one topic may appear in more than one paragraph.)

THE OLYMPIC GAMES

 I. Overview of the Olympic games.
   A. Ancient Greece   ( )
   B. Modern times   ( )
 II. Honor of winning or special moments
   A. Ancient Greece   ( )
   B. Modern times   ( )
III. Problems of the Olympics
   A. Political conflicts
      1. Ancient Greece   ( )
      2. Modern times   ( )
   B. Professionalism and specialization
      1. Ancient Greece   ( )
      2. Modern times   ( )

C. Following is another way to organize the same information. Find the missing topics in the reading and write them on the appropriate lines. The letters in parentheses refer to the lettered paragraphs of the reading.

 I. Ancient Greece

   A. _____ (A)

   B. _____ (B)

   C. _____ (E)

   D. _____ (B)

II. _____

    A. Overview of the Olympic games   (C)

    B. _____ (D)

    C. _____ (E)

    D. _____ (F)

D. Several of the topics include detailed examples. Find the examples of the following topics in the selection and write them on the appropriate lines.

There have been many special Olympic moments.

a. _____

b. _____

Politics have often influenced the games in modern times.

a. _____

b. _____

c. _____

d. _____

There have been problems with modern Olympic athletes.

a. _____

b. _____

Understanding Details

A. Find the following sentences in the reading selection. Which words do the underlined words refer to? Write them on the lines.

PARAGRAPH A

1. This celebration was held regularly every four years.
    an ancient Greek festival for athletes

2. These games were simpler than our modern ones. _____

_____

PARAGRAPH B

3. At <u>that time</u>, winning at a sport brought the highest possible honor to the individual competitor. _____

4. Because of <u>this interest</u> in money, the ancient games lost their original purpose. _____

PARAGRAPH C

5. The first of the modern Olympics took place in the <u>same country</u> as the original festivals. _____

PARAGRAPH D

6. To do <u>this</u>, he had to run the seven hundred miles to St. Louis. _____

    _____

7. As Jesse Owens received his medals, the <u>ruler of Germany</u> stared coldly from his seat. _____

PARAGRAPH E

8. Unfortunately, such has not been <u>the case</u> in modern times. _____

    _____

9. World war stopped the celebration of the Olympics in 1916, and the <u>same thing</u> happened in 1940 and 1944. _____

10. Because of South African politics, people continue to argue over the participation of athletes from <u>that country</u>. _____

    _____

PARAGRAPH F

11. <u>Some</u> have used illegal drugs and chemicals. _____

    _____

12. The line between "amateur" and "professional" can be a thin <u>one</u>.

    _____

B. Circle the letters of *all* the correct phrases for each of the following blanks.

1. The ancient Olympic games _____ .

    a. began in 1776 B.C.
    b. were held every four years
    c. were not held in time of war
    d. were open to men and women of many countries

2. The athletes in the very first Olympic game _____ .

    a. lived at the gymnasium in Olympia for years before competing
    b. ran in a one-foot race
    c. competed in six to ten different events
    d. participated in the games for the honor of it

3. The ancient Olympic games _____ .

    a. reached their height in the fifth century B.C.
    b. offered a reward of gold to the winner
    c. were open only to amateur athletes until after the fifth century B.C.
    d. never allowed professionals to compete

4. The modern Olympics _____ .

    a. first took place in 1936
    b. are spectacular events
    c. have competitors from over 100 countries
    d. are always held in Athens

5. Both Felix Carvajal and Jesse Owens _____ .

    a. were runners
    b. ran seven hundred miles to win gold medals
    c. competed in the 1904 Olympics
    d. were Cuban

6. Problems in the modern Olympics include _____ .

    a. politics
    b. the cost of gold medals
    c. the use of drugs
    d. professional specialization

Now turn back to the "Preparing to Read" section on page 163 and answer the questions.

Discussing the Reading

Talk about your answers to the following questions.

1. Have you ever attended the Olympics? If so, where and when?
2. Have you ever watched the Olympics on TV? When? What was your favorite event? How did you feel about the games?
3. Does your country send athletes to the Olympics? If so, what events do they compete in?
4. Can you think of answers to any of the problems of the modern Olympics?

PART TWO

DANGEROUS SPORTS

Glancing at Vocabulary (optional)

Here are some vocabulary items from the next reading selection. You can learn them now or come back to them later.

Nouns	Adjectives	Expressions
daredevil	dangerous	mountain climbing
adventure	afraid	scuba diving
ocean	scared	hang gliding
fear	normal	mental health

Verbs	Adverb
reach	slightly
glide	
check	

Skimming for Main Ideas

> The title of a paragraph should tell the main topic. Here are three topics:
> A "Normal" Kind of Daredevil
> The Adventure of Dangerous Sports
> A Chemical Cause

A. Read the following three paragraphs quickly and then match each paragraph with its correct topic. Write the topic title on the line.

Dangerous Sports

 A _____

For most people, playing tennis or going to the gym is a good way to exercise and relax. However, some people are not satisfied with such "boring" sports. They prefer dangerous sports like mountain climbing, scuba diving, or hang gliding. These daredevils love the adventure of reaching the top of the highest mountain, swimming underwater in dangerous areas of the ocean, or jumping off a mountain and silently gliding down to flat land. They feel most "alive" when there is the possibility that they might die the next minute.

B _____

   Why do these people participate in such dangerous sports? There are many answers. Some daredevils are actually very careful. They examine the potential dangers, pay attention to both their physical and mental health, and carefully check their equipment. Often, they choose a specific sport because they have always been frightened of it, and they want to have power over their fear. They do not want to die, but they do not want to be scared of dying either.

C _____

   Other daredevils are very different from "normal" people. Most people, for example, feel nervous before doing something dangerous, afraid during the event, and excited afterward. Many daredevils, on the other hand, feel so excited *during* the dangerous action that they decide to do it again and again. They are addicted to excitement as other people are addicted to drugs or alcohol. It is possible that many daredevils have slightly higher amounts of certain chemicals in their bodies, but scientists haven't studied this enough yet to be sure.

B. Answer the following questions about the previous three paragraphs. Then put together the answers to write the main idea.

PARAGRAPH A

1. Who is the paragraph about? *people who like adventure*
2. What do these people do? *participate in dangerous sports*
3. What is the main idea of the paragraph? *some people who like adventure participate in dangerous sports*

PARAGRAPH B

4. Who is the paragraph about? _____
5. Are these people very different from other people? _____
6. What is the main idea of the paragraph? _____

_____

PARAGRAPH C

7. Who is the paragraph about? _____
8. Why do these people do dangerous things? _____

_____

9. What is the main idea of the paragraph? _____

_____

Now reread the three paragraphs. Try to guess the meaning of the new words from the context. Use your dictionary only when absolutely necessary. Then complete the following exercise.

Inferring: Figuring Out the Meaning

Write a 1 on the line in front of the ideas that the author clearly stated, a 2 before the ideas that the writer simply implied, and a 3 before the ideas that are not in the reading at all. Look back at the reading if necessary.

1. __*1*__   Some people find playing tennis or exercising in the gym boring.

2. _____   Mountain climbing, scuba diving, and hang gliding are dangerous activities.

3. _____   A person could die from participation in certain sports.

4. _____   Daredevil sports are excellent for the health.

5. _____   Some people are very careful when they participate in dangerous sports.

6. _____   Most choose sports that they know they are good at.

7. _____   Many daredevils have a feeling of excitement while they are doing dangerous acts.

8. _____   People can be addicted to feelings as well as to chemicals.

9. _____   Doctors can treat addiction to danger with drugs.

Discussing the Reading

Talk about your answers to the following questions.

1. What sports do you enjoy watching? What sports do you enjoy playing?
2. Have you ever been interested in a dangerous sport? If so, which one? Why?
3. What are you afraid of? What do you do about this fear?
4. What is the most dangerous thing that you have ever done? How did you feel about it?

PART THREE

BUILDING VOCABULARY; STUDY SKILLS

A. Cross out the word in each group that doesn't belong. Explain your decisions.

1. professional	2. wrestling	3. frightened	4. festival
daredevil	reading	fear	competition
athlete	jumping	scared	gymnasium
~~medal~~	running	afraid	games

5. reward	6. amateur	7. tennis	8. gold
crown	participant	scuba diving	leaves
dangerous	competitor	mountain climbing	silver
honor	adventure	hang gliding	money

B. Circle the letters of *all* the possible words for each blank.

1. Twelve _____ ran in the race.

   a. athletes   b. competitors   c. spectators   d. runners

2. She enjoys _____ sports.

   a. amateur   b. fear   c. dangerous   d. afraid

3. He competed in the _____ .

   a. café   b. event   c. marathon   d. footrace

Study Skill: Prediction

> Because good reading requires an active mind, fluent readers make "predictions" about the material they are reading. They try to quickly guess—without thinking about it—what is going to come next.

The following exercise will improve your ability to predict. In each sentence, complete or fill in the last word. (There can be more than one correct answer.) Work as fast as you can. At the end of each section, write your time (how many seconds it took you to complete the exercise.)

1. Athletes competed in sports festi_____ .

2. What is your native lan_____ .

3. Discus throwing is an Olympic ev_____ .

4. The race was five mi_____ .

5. The American Jesse Owens won a gold me_____ .

Time: _____

6. A daredevil might die in the next min_____ .

7. Some athletes use illegal dr_____ .

8. Do you play ten_____ ?

9. Do you have the spirit of adven_____ ?

10. Have you ever climbed to the top of a moun_____ ?

Time: _____

11. I'm still hungry. May I have a second serv_____ ?

12. People used to believe that witches flew on broom_____ .

13. The Romans had a celebration at the time of the har_____ .

14. On Halloween, children dress up in cos_____ .

15. What are some special holiday cus_____ ?

Time: _____

16. The Celts held a festival for the Lord of the Dead at the beginning of

_____ .

17. I accepted an invitation to a dinner _____ .

18. The next day, you should send the hostess a thank-you _____ .

19. Should I bring candy, flowers, or some other _____ ?

20. My roommate joined a computer dating _____ .

Time: _____

21. I met a guy in the produce section of the _____ .

22. Carefully fill out the application _____ .

23. We've been talking about marriage, friendship, and other _____ .

24. I don't go to a gym because I hate to _____ .

25. Do you buy the products from TV _____ ?

Time: _____

PART FOUR

SCANNING FOR INFORMATION

When we go to a college sports event, we usually get a program that lists the athletes and some information about them. Look at the list of college football players on pages 178 and 179, and answer the questions about them as fast as you can.

Here are some abbreviations used in sports programs:

Pos. = position on the team   Sr. = senior (fourth year)
Fr. = freshman (first year in college)   C = center (position on the team)
So. = sophomore (second year)   LG = left guard
Jr. = junior (third year)   ILB = inside line backer

1. How are the names of the team members arranged? _____

2. What does "No." (at the top of each column) mean? _____

    What does Hgt. mean? _____ What does Wgt. mean? _____

3. What are four different abbreviations for the names of positions? _____
    _____

4. UCLA is located in Los Angeles, California. How many players on the UCLA

    team are from Los Angeles? _____

5. Is the number on Jim Mastera's uniform 90? _____ Is he a guard? _____ Is he

    from California? _____ How do you know? _____

6. What is the number on Steve Davis' uniform? _____ What position does Steve

    play? _____ How tall is he? _____ How much does he weigh? _____

    What class is he in? _____ Where is he from? _____

7. Who is Number 15? _____

    What year of school is he in? _____

8. Which player is from another country? _____

9. How many players have three varsity letters? _____

10. Who is the heaviest player on the team? _____ Who is the

    lightest? _____ The tallest? _____

Going Beyond the Text

Bring to class programs from sports events that you have attended. Write the abbreviations and new vocabulary on the board. Discuss them.

Use the vocabulary, with additional words, to describe the sport. Read the rules for a sport. Summarize them for the class.

UCLA   Alphabetical Roster

No.	Name	Pos.	Hgt.	Wgt.	Class	Hometown
73	Alexander, Jim	LG	6-4½	247	Fr.	Pinole
14	Alexander, Kirk	SE	5-11	177	Fr.	Santa Monica
83	Anderson, Willie	FL	5-11¾	154	Fr.	Paulsboro, NJ
24	**Andrews, Danny	TB	5-10¾	175	Jr.	Carson
43	Armstrong, Sean	SS	5-11½	190	Fr.	Rowland Heights
	Baaden, Steve	QB	5-10¾	193	So.	Torrance
71	**Baran, Dave	C	6-5½	267	Jr.	Newfield, NJ
92	Batchkoff, Frank	DRT	6-4½	238	Fr.	Reseda
94	**Bergmann, Paul	TE	6-2¼	233	Sr.	Canoga Park
78	Block, Chris	NG	6-3¼	256	Jr.	Valencia
91	Bolin, Greg	TE	6-1¾	230	Fr.	Fountain Valley
12	**Bono, Steve	QB	6-3¾	210	Jr.	Norristown, PA
17	**Buenafe, Kevin	P	6-0	205	Jr.	Tulare
86	***Butler, Ron	ILB	6-2¼	229	Sr.	Greenville, NC
46	***Cephous, Frank	FB	5-10¾	220	Sr.	Neward, DE
44	*Chaffin, Jeff	DLT	6-3½	255	Sr.	Santa Barbara
	Clark, Brian	NG	6-2	225	Fr.	Inglewood
19	Clinton, David	SE	5-7	180	Fr.	Lomita
76	Cox, Chris	LT	6-5¼	235	Fr.	St. Louis, MO
45	Craig, Paco	FL	5-10	161	Fr.	Riverside
6	***Crawford, Lyndon	RC	6-0½	198	Sr.	Chicago, IL
65	Cronin, Kevin	RT	6-4¼	255	Jr.	La Crescenta
62	Davis, Steve	C	6-4¾	221	Fr.	Clovis
39	**Dellocono, Neal	OLB	6-0¾	222	Jr.	Baton Rouge, LA
27	Dial, Alan	TB	6-0¼	173	Fr.	Anniston, AL
	Dias, Bob	SE	5-10½	175	Sr.	Fullerton
31	*Donatelli, Doug	OLB	6-2	203	Sr.	Manhattan Beach
8	*Dorrell, Karl	FL	5-11	186	So.	San Diego
	Elsea, Chris	DB	5-9½	185	Fr.	Los Alamitos
33	Francois, Greg	FB	5-10¼	195	Fr.	Alexandria, VA
	Franey, Dave	PK	5-8½	160	Fr.	Kansas City, MO
87	Franklin, Scott	TE	6-1¾	194	So.	Santa Ana
20	Garibaldi, Bob	TB	5-10 ¼	184	Fr.	Stockton
28	*Gasser, Joe	SS	5-10½	180	So.	Torrance
74	***Gemza, Steve	LT	6-8	275	Sr.	Dayton, OH
58	Glasser, Jeff	DLT	6-3½	235	Fr.	Houston, TX
69	Goebel, Joe	C	6-5¾	250	Fr.	Midland, TX
72	*Gordon, Scott	RT	6-4½	256	Sr.	Bremerton, WA
	Greuner, Mike	OLB	5-10½	186	Jr.	Berlin, West Germany
	Hackett, Kyle	SE	5-9½	181	Sr.	Sacramento
63	*Hartmeier, Mike	LG	6-5	266	So.	Salinas
36	Henderson, Ted	P	6-2	186	So.	Albuquerque, NM
97	***Howell, Harper	TE	6-3¼	225	Sr.	Boulder, CO
	Hudspeth, Marcus	DL	6-3¼	228	Jr.	Los Angeles
57	Hutchins, Adam	ILB	6-1¾	225	Fr.	Las Vegas, NV
	Irvine, Gifford	FL	5-6	149	Fr.	Los Angeles
59	Jackson, Melvin	OLB	6-3½	222	Fr.	Suffolk, VA
99	*Jarecki, Steve	OLB	6-2¼	225	So.	Napa
54	Jordon, Wes	NG	6-2¾	223	Fr.	Redondo Beach
70	Kidder, John	RT	6-5	269	Fr.	Encino
85	*Knowles, Lee	ILB	6-1¼	223	Jr.	Huntington Beach
	Kordakis, Jim	QB	5-11¾	191	Sr.	Van Nuys
25	*Lee, John	PK	5-10¾	175	So.	Downey
	Lower, Scott	SE	5-10	153	So.	Denver, CO

*Indicates number of UCLA varsity letters, won.

UCLA Alphabetical Roster

No.	Name	Pos.	Hgt.	Wgt.	Class	Hometown
67	**Love, Duval	LT	6-2¾	273	Jr.	Fountain Valley
96	Mahan, Mike	ILB	6-3	237	Jr.	Bell
56	*Mannon, Mark	C	6-4	250	Jr.	Santa Barbara
90	Mastera, Jim	ILB	6-2½	230	Fr.	Cherry Hill, NJ
77	*McCullough, Jim	RG	6-5¼	267	So.	Hemet
	McGaugh, Eugene	FB	5-11¼	205	Fr.	Simi Valley
	McLaughlin, Tom	QB	5-11¼	183	Jr.	Holbrook, NY
81	**Mewborn, Gene	ILB	6-2½	232	Sr.	Lexington, MA
48	Miller, Chuckie	RC	5-8½	167	Fr.	Long Beach
15	Moore, Terry	OLB	6-0¼	200	Jr.	St. Louis, MO
3	***Nelson, Kevin	TB	5-10½	196	Sr.	Los Angeles
10	**Neuheisel, Rick	QB	6-0½	192	Sr.	Tempe, AZ
9	*Norrie, David	QB	6-4¾	220	So.	Portland, OR
50	Nowinski, Jeff	ILB	6-3¼	231	Fr.	Whittier
96	**Page, Kenny	DRT	6-3½	238	Sr.	Colorado Spgs, CO
55	Pankopf, Tory	NG	6-2¾	238	Fr.	Long Beach
48	*Phillips, Tony	OLB	6-0	210	So.	Santa Monica
93	Pickert, Joe	TE	6-4	218	Fr.	Kansas City, KS
47	**Pitts, Ron	RC	5-10	180	Jr.	Orchard Park, NY
4	*Potter, Ken	PK	6-1	207	Jr.	Alta Loma
42	Price, Dennis	LC	6-0½	158	Fr.	Long Beach
37	Primus, James	TB	5-10½	185	Fr.	National City
64	*Randle, David	DLT	6-3½	237	Jr.	Dallas, TX
	Renner, Terry	TE	6-1¾	194	Fr.	Mission Viejo
7	***Rogers, Don	FS	6-1¼	206	Sr.	Sacramento
61	Rogers, Eric	RT	6-3¾	266	Fr.	Colton
	Rozsa, David	LB	6-2¼	216	Fr.	Los Angeles
	Rozsa, Doug	LB	6-2¼	219	Fr.	Los Angeles
30	Rutledge, Craig	FS	6-0½	184	Fr.	Placentia
21	***Sanchez, Lupe	LC	5-9¼	187	Sr.	Visalia
82	*Sherrard, Mike	SE	6-1¾	185	So.	Chico
32	*Shinnick, Josh	FS	5-11¾	191	So.	Columbia, MO
53	Simpson, David	ILB	6-0½	192	Fr.	Pomona
	Smith, Bob	QB	6-0½	188	Fr.	Los Angeles
68	Smith, Earl	RG	6-1¼	245	So.	Los Angeles
11	Stevens, Matt	QB	5-11½	200	Fr.	Fountain Valley
51	*Taylor, Tommy	ILB	6-0½	238	Sr.	Chattanooga, TN
23	Tennell, Derek	FB	6-4½	225	Fr.	West Covina
78	*Theodore, Terry	C	6-1½	221	So.	Sunnyvale
	Thompson, Terry	OLB	5-11	205	So.	Costa Mesa
	Thropay, Reuben	ILB	6-2¾	201	So.	Montebello
40	Tumey, Terry	NG	6-1¾	221	Fr.	Tulsa, OK
	Van Remortel, Fred	DB	5-11¾	182	So.	Los Angeles
95	*Walen, Mark	DRT	6-5	245	So.	Burlingame
29	Washington, James	LC	6-0¾	185	Fr.	Los Angeles
75	Wassel, Doug	DRT	6-3½	228	Fr.	Georgetown, PA
2	Welch, Herb	RC	5-10¾	175	Jr.	Cerritos
41	**West, Doug	OLB	6-3¾	214	Sr.	Del Mar
22	**Wiley, Bryan	FB	6-1	206	Jr.	Harbor City
60	**Williams, Steve	LG	6-2¾	243	Sr.	Yorba Linda
56	Wilson, Al	FL	6-0¼	175	Jr.	Carson
36	Wilson, Leonard	TB	5-9¼	182	Fr.	Ft. Lauderdale, FL
66	***Yelch, Chris	RG	6-4	284	Sr.	La Porte, IN
18	**Young, Mike	FL	6-1¼	185	Jr.	Visalia
79	Zweneveid, Onno	RT	6-4¾	261	Fr.	Canoga Park

PART FIVE

PERSONAL STORIES

Follow these steps for the story:

1. Read it quickly and tell the main idea.
2. Answer your instructor's questions about the story, or ask and answer questions of your own.
3. Tell your own opinions of the ideas in the story.
4. Tell or write about your own experience with sports.

The Sporting Life

I come from the most competitive, athletic family you can imagine. Everyone in my family participates in sports—except me. My parents are good swimmers and scuba divers. My brother is a professional tennis player. My sister is a runner; she's only fifteen, but she's already won medals in several races, and she's preparing for a marathon next year. One of my uncles is a mountain climber, and two of my cousins are very good at hang gliding. Unfortunately, I've never been athletic at all—I'm the least athletic person I know. My favorite "sport" is reading.

Nevertheless, last year I decided to try to learn a sport. I wanted to have something in common with the rest of my family. Although I'm a terrible swimmer, I decided to take sailing lessons. Why? I enjoy the ocean, and I thought, "I won't have to exercise very much."

Well, the first lesson was good. It was in a classroom. However, the second lesson was actually on a sailboat. At first, everything was fine. We put the sail up. Good. We untied the boat. Okay. We slowly moved out of the marina to the ocean. Fine. But then it happened. A strong wind hit us, and we were suddenly gliding through the water—very fast. Moreover, the wind caught our sail and tipped the boat over to one side, very close to the water. "I'm going to die!" I thought.

"Isn't this dangerous?" I asked the instructor.

He looked surprised and said, "Oh, *no*. This is exciting. This is adventure! This is *living!*"

Well, that was my last sailing lesson. Now I stay on the beach to participate in my favorite sport—opening a good book.

12

YOU, THE CONSUMER

ADVERTISING: THE SELLING OF A PRODUCT

Getting Started

Look at the picture and talk about it.

1. Where is the person? What is he trying to do?
2. Why is he confused?
3. What kind of product is he looking at?
4. Do you think these products are similar to one another or different from one another?

Preparing to Read

Think about the answers to the following questions. (The reading selection will answer them.)

1. What influences us when we decide to buy one product instead of another?
2. What kind of information do we get from advertising?
3. What methods do advertisers use to sell products?
4. Who is not affected by advertising?

Glancing at Vocabulary (optional)

Here are some vocabulary items from the reading selection. You can answer them now or come back to them later.

Nouns	Verbs	Expressions
consumer	pick	instead of
advertisement (ad)	admit	on the market
consumerism	prevent	self-image
advertiser	realize	get . . . to
price		
advertising	**Adjectives**	
color	complete	
package	stupid	

Read the following selection quickly. Then answer the questions after the reading.

Advertising: The Selling of a Product

A   A consumer walks into a store. He stands in front of hundreds of boxes of laundry detergent. He chooses one brand, pays for it, and leaves. Why does he pick that specific kind of soap? Is it truly better than the others? Probably not. These days, many products are nearly identical to one another in quality and price. If products are almost the same, what makes consumers buy one brand instead of another? Although we might not like to admit it, commercials on television and advertisements in magazines probably influence us much more than we think they do.

B   Advertising informs consumers about new products available on the market. It gives us information about everything from shampoo to toothpaste to computers and cars. But there is one serious problem with this. The "information" is actually very often "*mis*information." It tells us the products' benefits but hides their disadvantages. Advertising not only leads us to buy things that we don't need and can't afford, but it also confuses our sense of reality. "Zoom toothpaste prevents cavities and gives you white teeth!" the advertisement tells us. But it doesn't tell us the complete truth: that a healthy diet and a good toothbrush will have the same effect.

C   Advertisers use many methods to get us to buy their products. One of their most successful methods is to make us feel dissatisfied with ourselves and our imperfect lives. Advertisements show us who we aren't and what we don't have. Our teeth aren't white enough. Our hair isn't shiny enough. Our clothes aren't clean enough. Advertisements make us afraid that people won't like us if we don't use the advertised products. "Why don't I have any dates?" a good-looking girl sadly asks in a commercial. "Here," replies her roommate, "try Zoom toothpaste!" Of course she tries it, and immediately the whole football team falls in love with her. "That's a stupid commercial," we might say. But we still buy Zoom toothpaste out of fear of being unpopular and having no friends.

D   If fear is the negative motive for buying a product, then wanting a good self-image is the positive reason for choosing it. Each of us has a mental picture of the kind of person we would like to be. For example, a modern young woman might like to think that she looks like a beautiful movie star. A middle-aged man might want to see himself as a strong, attractive athlete. Advertisers know this. They write specific ads to make certain groups of people choose their product. Two people may choose different brands of toothpaste with the identical price, amount, and quality; each person believes that he or she is expressing his personality by choosing that brand.

E   Advertisers get psychologists to study the way consumers think and their reasons for choosing one brand instead of another. These experts tell advertisers about the motives of fear and self-image. They also inform them about recent studies with colors and words. Psychologists have found that certain colors on the package of an attractive product will cause people to reach out and take that package instead of buying an identical product with different colors. Also, certain words attract our attention. For example, the words "new," "improved," "natural," and "giant size" are very popular and seem to pull our eyes and hand toward the package.

F   Many people believe that advertising does not affect them. They know that there is freedom to choose, and they like to think they make wise choices. Unfortunately, they probably don't realize the powerful effect of advertising. They may not clearly understand that advertisers spend billions of dollars each year in aggressive competition for our money, and they are extremely successful. Do you believe that ads don't influence your choice of products? Just look at the brands in your kitchen and bathroom.

Getting the Main Ideas

Write T (true), F (false), or I (impossible to know from the reading) on the lines.

1. _____   Advertising influences us to buy one kind of product instead of another.

2. _____   Advertisements always provide us with important information about products.

3. _____   Wanting a good self-image is a powerful reason for choosing products.

4. _____   If you use Zoom toothpaste, there will be no more problems in your life.

5. _____   The "Psychology of Selling" is an important course in many business colleges.

Guessing Meaning from Context

A. Try to use the context clues to write more and more specific definitions of the underlined word in each of the following sentences.

1. A consumer buys <u>detergent</u>. *something to buy*

2. A consumer buys a box of laundry <u>detergent</u>. *something to buy that comes in a box and is for laundry*

3. A consumer buys a box of laundry <u>detergent</u>. Why does he or she pick that specific kind of soap? _____

_____

*   *   *

4. You choose one <u>brand</u>. _____

5. You choose one <u>brand</u> of detergent, toothpaste, or shampoo.

_____

6. You choose one <u>brand</u> of detergent, toothpaste, or shampoo because of TV commercials and magazine advertisements for that kind of product. _____

_____

B. Circle the words that give clues to the meaning of the underlined word in each of the following sentences. Then write a definition of each word on the line. Check your answer in a dictionary.

1. These days, many products are nearly <u>identical</u> to one another in quality and price. If they are almost the same, what makes us buy one brand instead of another? _____

_____

2. Advertising <u>informs</u> us about new products available on the market, but it tells us only of their benefits. _____

_____

3. Advertising gives us information about products, but there is a problem: The "information" is actually very often <u>misinformation</u>. _____

4. "Zoom toothpaste prevents <u>cavities</u> and gives you white teeth!" the advertisement tells us. _____

_____

5. If fear is the negative <u>motive</u> for buying a product, then wanting a good self-image is the positive reason for choosing it.

    _____

6. Advertisers regularly get <u>psychologists</u> to study the way consumers think and their motives for choosing one brand instead of another.

    _____

7. Certain words attract our attention. For example, the words "new and improved" are very popular and seem to pull our eyes and hands toward an <u>attractive</u> package.

    _____

Recognizing Reading Structure

1. On the lines write the main idea of the reading.

    _____

    _____

2. Outline the selection by writing the main ideas on the appropriate lines. The words in parentheses are the main topics—cues to help you; the letters in parentheses at the ends of the lines refer to the lettered paragraphs in the reading.

    I. (Introduction) _____ (A)

    II. (Misinformation of advertising) _____

    _____ (B)

        a. (Benefits of products) _____

        b. (Disadvantages) _____

        c. (Reality) _____

    III. (Methods of advertisers) _____

    _____

        a. (Fear) _____ (C)

        b. (Self-image) _____ (D)

        c. (Colors and words) _____ (E)

    IV. (Conclusion) _____ (F)

Understanding Details

Sometimes a writer exaggerates (makes something seem more than it really is) or uses humor to make a point. The reader knows that the information is not exactly true but understands the author's reason for exaggerating.

Example: "Zoom toothpaste prevents cavities and gives you white teeth!" (There is no toothpaste called Zoom; the author intends, humorously, for the name to suggest speed, modernity, and other qualities of "wonderful" products.)

A. Circle the letter that indicates the "real meaning" of each of the following sentences.

1. This product makes clothes whiter than white!

   a. This product is only for clothes that are white.
   b. This product will clean clothes well.
   c. This product will change the color of clothes.

2. Our teeth aren't white enough. Our hair isn't shiny enough. Our clothes aren't clean enough.

   a. We should wash our clothes with toothpaste and shampoo.
   b. To improve ourselves, we should immediately buy the products in the commercials.
   c. We should go to a psychologist to talk about our problems.

3. In the commercial, she tries Zoom toothpaste, and immediately the whole football team falls in love with her.

   a. According to commercials, people will like you better if you use their products.
   b. Zoom toothpaste is the best in the world.
   c. Football players often fall in love with actresses in commercials.

4. A modern young woman might like to think that she looks like a beautiful movie star.

   a. A modern young woman wants to be as attractive as possible.
   b. Every modern young woman wants to act in movies.
   c. Most modern women think that they are beautiful.

5. A middle-aged man might want to see himself as a strong, attractive athlete.

   a. All middle-aged men are in good physical health.
   b. Older men should all get exercise in the gym.
   c. Men usually want to look as attractive as possible.

B. Circle the letters of *all* the correct phrases for each of the following blanks.

1. Advertising _____ .

   a. informs us about some products
   b. doesn't influence us very much
   c. misinforms us
   d. doesn't always tell us everything about a product

2. A person often buys a product because _____ .

   a. he or she is dissatisfied with himself or herself
   b. of a need for a good self-image
   c. of the colors on the package
   d. of certain words on the package

3. Advertisers _____ to make us buy products.

   a. offer very low prices
   b. get information from psychologists
   c. spend a lot of money
   d. need to use better detergent and shampoo

4. Psychologists tell advertisers _____ .

   a. which brands of toothpaste to produce
   b. to stop influencing shoppers
   c. about people's motives for buying
   d. how much money to spend on television commercials

5. The words _____ on products are very popular and seem to attract our attention.

   a. "really cheap"
   b. "natural"
   c. "improved"
   d. "good enough"

Now turn back to the "Preparing to Read" section on page 183 and answer the questions.

Discussing the Reading

Talk about your answers to the following questions.

1. What kinds of advertising attracts your attention? Do you sometimes buy the products in the ads or commercials?
2. How are American and Canadian advertisements and commercials different from those in your country?
3. Are there any rules or laws about advertising in your country?

4. What image would you like to have for yourself? Would you like to be similar to any people you see in television commercials or magazine ads?
5. What famous brands of products do you have in your home now? Why did you buy these?

PART TWO

SMART SHOPPING

Glancing at Vocabulary (optional)

Here are some vocabulary items from the next reading selection. You can learn them now or come back to them later.

Nouns	Adjectives	Expressions
advice	generic	grocery store
manufacturer	discount	small print
	plain	on sale
Verb		name brands
compare		dressing room

Skimming for Main Ideas

Read each of the following three paragraphs quickly. Then write the main idea of each paragraph on the line.

Smart Shopping

A   ADVICE FOR CONSUMERS

Most mothers have a good piece of advice: Never go into a supermarket hungry! If you go shopping for food before lunchtime, you'll probably buy more than you plan to. Unfortunately, however, just this advice isn't enough for consumers these days. Modern shoppers need an education in how—and how not—to buy things at the grocery store. First, you should check the weekly newspaper ads. Find out the items that are on sale and decide if you really need those things. In other words, don't buy anything just because it's cheaper than usual! Next, in the market, carefully read the information on the package, and don't let words like "New and Improved!" or "All Natural" on the front of a package influence you. Instead, read the list of ingredients on the back. Third, compare prices; that is, you should examine the prices of both different brands and different sizes of the same brand.

The main idea: _____

_____

B   GENERIC ITEMS AND BRAND NAMES

Another suggestion for consumers is to buy generic items instead of famous brands. Generic items in supermarkets come in plain packages. These products are cheaper because manufacturers don't spend much money on packaging or advertising. The quality, however, is usually identical to the quality of well-known name brands. In the same way, in buying clothes, you can often find high quality and low prices in brands that are not famous. Shopping in discount clothing stores can also help you save a lot of money. Although these stores aren't very attractive, and they usually do not have individual dressing rooms, not only are the prices low, but you can often find the same famous brands that you find in high-priced department stores.

The main idea: _____

_____

C   INTELLIGENT CONSUMERISM

Wise consumers read magazine advertisements and watch TV commercials, but they do this with one advantage: knowledge of the psychology behind the ads. In other words, well-informed consumers watch for information and check for misinformation. They ask themselves questions: Is the advertiser hiding something in small print at the bottom of the page? Is there any real information in the commercial, or is the advertiser simply showing an attractive image? Is this product more expensive than it should be because it has a famous name? With the answers to these questions, consumers can make a wise choice.

The main idea: _____

_____

Now reread the three paragraphs. Try to guess meanings of new words from their context. Use your dictionary only when absolutely necessary. Then complete the following exercises.

Viewpoint

Complete the following sentence.

The author of the reading selection implies her point of view. Her opinion of advertising is that _____

_____

_____

_____

Inferring: Figuring Out the Meaning

Write a 1 on the line in front of the ideas that the author clearly stated; a 2 before the ideas that the author simply implied; and a 3 before the ideas that are not in the reading at all. Look back at the selection if necessary.

1. ____   People who shop for groceries when they are hungry usually buy more than people who shop after dinner.

2. ____   Items on sale are cheaper than usual.

3. ____   It's a good idea to read the ingredients on the back of a package.

4. ____   Sometimes it's better to buy one size of a product than another.

5. ____   Generic items never say "New and Improved! All Natural!"

6. ____   Generic products are usually cheaper than famous brands.

7. ____   To save money, you should buy clothes in discount stores rather than expensive department stores.

8. ____   An intelligent shopper knows something about consumer psychology.

Discussing the Reading

Talk about your answers to the following questions.

1. Has your mother ever given you any advice about shopping? If so, what was the advice?
2. Do you buy generic items? Why or why not?
3. How is shopping in North America different from shopping in your country?
4. What advice can you give a foreigner who wants to go shopping in your country?

PART THREE

BUILDING VOCABULARY; STUDY SKILLS

Some adjectives consist of two or more words, often connected by a hyphen. These adjectives usually end in *-ing* or *-ed*.

Examples: a *high-priced* store (a store with high prices); a *well-known* detective (a detective who many people know about)

A. Write the missing adjectives in the blanks. Choose from these:

good-looking	English-speaking	sweet-tasting	modern-thinking
well-informed	well-known	low-priced	long-lived

1. I buy _____ clothes in discount stores because I can't afford the expensive name brands.

2. _____ shoppers know about the prices and the quality of products.

3. We all want a positive self-image: We think that a _____ person should buy certain products.

4. Do the _____ people of healthful mountain areas need to buy medicines and chemicals to improve their lives?

5. Consumers prefer _____ toothpaste: Thus they buy brands with sugar in them.

6. I saw a _____ movie star in the department store the other day.

7. _____ young consumers buy clothes and products that will improve their image.

8. Advertising on most TV channels in the United States is for _____ consumers, but some is for people who speak other languages.

B. Without using a dictionary, match each word on the left with its meaning on the right. Write the correct letter on the line.

1. _d_ pick
2. ____ brand
3. ____ nearly
4. ____ consumer
5. ____ supermarket
6. ____ attractive
7. ____ psychologist
8. ____ on sale
9. ____ suggestion

a. person who studies the way people think
b. shopper
c. piece of advice
d. choose; select
e. cheaper than usual
f. kind; specific name of a product
g. grocery store
h. almost
i. good-looking

C. Circle the letters of *all* the words that might fit in each blank.

1. There weren't many ＿＿＿＿＿＿＿ in the small grocery store.

   a. products   b. brands   c. motives   d. choices

2. He ＿＿＿＿＿＿＿ several products.

   a. informed   b. compared   c. picked   d. attracted

3. The ＿＿＿＿＿＿＿ discussed the psychology of the ads.

   a. manufacturers   b. advertisers   c. cavities   d. consumers

4. Their motives were ＿＿＿＿＿＿＿ .

   a. identical   b. generic   c. discount   d. stupid

5. They gave me some very good ＿＿＿＿＿＿＿ .

   a. detergent   b. advice   c. misinformation   d. suggestions

Study Skill: Using a Dictionary (Word Usage)

All the words in the following exercise appeared in this chapter's readings. They are used differently in these sentences, however. If possible, everyone in the class should use the same kind of dictionary for this exercise. Work quickly. The first student with the correct answers is the winner. Look up the following underlined words. Write the part of speech and the appropriate definition for each word as it is used in the sentence.

1. I don't <u>date</u> much, probably because I don't use the right shampoo. ＿＿＿＿＿＿＿

   ＿＿＿＿＿＿＿＿＿＿＿＿＿＿＿＿＿＿＿＿＿＿＿＿＿＿＿＿＿＿＿＿＿＿＿＿＿＿＿

2. She <u>zoomed</u> out of the house to buy the product that she saw on TV. ＿＿＿＿＿＿

   ＿＿＿＿＿＿＿＿＿＿＿＿＿＿＿＿＿＿＿＿＿＿＿＿＿＿＿＿＿＿＿＿＿＿＿＿＿＿＿

3. I can't understand the <u>psychology</u> of people who buy only name brands. ＿＿＿＿

   ＿＿＿＿＿＿＿＿＿＿＿＿＿＿＿＿＿＿＿＿＿＿＿＿＿＿＿＿＿＿＿＿＿＿＿＿＿＿＿

4. I'm looking in the classified <u>ads</u> for a job. ＿＿＿＿＿＿＿＿＿＿＿＿＿＿＿

   ＿＿＿＿＿＿＿＿＿＿＿＿＿＿＿＿＿＿＿＿＿＿＿＿＿＿＿＿＿＿＿＿＿＿＿＿＿＿＿

5. Intelligence is his best <u>quality</u>. ＿＿＿＿＿＿＿＿＿＿＿＿＿＿＿＿＿＿＿＿＿

6. Never <u>discount</u> the importance of advertising. ＿＿＿＿＿＿＿＿＿＿＿＿＿＿

   ＿＿＿＿＿＿＿＿＿＿＿＿＿＿＿＿＿＿＿＿＿＿＿＿＿＿＿＿＿＿＿＿＿＿＿＿＿＿＿

7. Some <u>wise</u> guy in the department store tried to sell me shoes that were too small.

   ＿＿＿＿＿＿＿＿＿＿＿＿＿＿＿＿＿＿＿＿＿＿＿＿＿＿＿＿＿＿＿＿＿＿＿＿＿＿＿

PART FOUR
SCANNING FOR INFORMATION

As you have seen from this chapter, it is important for a consumer to carefully examine products. It is also important to understand the psychology of advertising.

Look at the following ads and answer the questions about them.

1.

2.

3.

4.

1. What product is advertised in the four ads? _____

2. What kind of person do you see in ad 1? _____

    How is he dressed? _____

    What might his profession be? _____

3. What kind of person do you see in ad 2? _____

    How is she dressed? _____

    What might her profession be? _____

    What does her body language tell you? _____

4. Where are the people in ad 3? _____

    How are they dressed? _____

    In your opinion, what kind of people might they be? _____

    _____

5. Where is the man in ad 4? _____

    How is he dressed? _____

    What four words in this ad might attract some people? _____

    _____

6. What is the self-image of a person who might be attracted to:

    ad 1 _____

    ad 2 _____

    ad 3 _____

    ad 4 _____

7. What does ad 3 lead the reader to think about the product?

    _____

    What misinformation can you find in ads 3 and 4? _____

    _____

Going Beyond the Text

In groups, look through magazines for advertisements about the same kind of product. List the brand names. List the words that are used in several or all the ads. Discuss them. What is their purpose? What image might they express? What kind of consumers do the ads want to attract? Then list the words that are in only one ad. How does this ad differ from other ads? Finally, listen to TV commercials. Which words are the same as in magazine ads? Which are different? Why?

PART FIVE

PERSONAL STORIES

Follow these steps for the story:

1. Read it quickly and tell the main idea.
2. Answer your instructor's questions about the story, or ask and answer questions of your own.
3. Tell your own opinions of the ideas in the story.
4. Tell or write about your own experiences with shopping.

Big Business

Back in my country, when I was a child, I used to go to "market day" with my mother. One day each week, farmers used to bring their fruit and vegetables into the city. They closed one street to all cars, and the farmers set up tables for their produce. This outdoor market was a great place to shop. Everything was fresher than produce in grocery stores because the farmers brought it in immediately after harvest. My mother and I always got there early in the morning to get the freshest produce.

The outdoor market was a wonderful adventure for a small child. It was like a festival—full of colors and sounds. There were red tomatoes, yellow lemons, green lettuce, peppers, grapes, onions. The farmers did their own advertising. They all shouted loudly for customers to buy their produce. "Come and buy my beautiful oranges! They're juicy and delicious and full of vitamins to make your children healthy and strong!"

Everyone used to argue with the farmers over the price of their produce. It was like a wonderful drama in a theater; the buyers and sellers were the "actors" in this drama. My mother was an expert at this. First, she picked the freshest, most attractive tomatoes, for example. Then she asked the price. The seller told her.

"What?" she said. She looked very surprised. "So expensive?"

The seller looked terribly hurt. "My dear lady!" he replied. "I am a poor, honest farmer. These are the cheapest tomatoes on the market!"

They always argued for several minutes before agreeing on a price. My mother took her tomatoes and left. Both buyer and seller were satisfied. The drama was over.